First World War
and Army of Occupation
War Diary
France, Belgium and Germany

29 DIVISION
86 Infantry Brigade
Duke of Cambridge's Own (Middlesex Regiment)
16th Battalion
24 April 1916 - 22 February 1918

WO95/2302/2

The Naval & Military Press Ltd
www.nmarchive.com
Published in association with The National Archives

Published by

The Naval & Military Press Ltd

Unit 10 Ridgewood Industrial Park,

Uckfield, East Sussex,

TN22 5QE England

Tel: +44 (0) 1825 749494

www.naval-military-press.com

www.nmarchive.com

Contents

Document type	Place/Title	Date From	Date To
Heading	WO95/2302/2		
Heading	29th Division 86th Infy Bde, 16th Bn Middx Regt Apr 1916-Feb 1918 From 33 Div 100 Bde.		
Heading	29th Division. 86th Infantry Brigade. 16th Battalion Middlesex Regiment April 1916		
War Diary		24/04/1916	28/04/1916
War Diary		08/05/1916	18/05/1916
Heading	29th Division. 86th Infantry Brigade. 16th Battalion Middlesex Regiment May 1916		
War Diary		08/05/1916	28/05/1916
Heading	29th Division. 86th Infantry Brigade. 16th Battalion Middlesex Regiment June 1916		
War Diary		07/06/1916	30/06/1916
Operation(al) Order(s)	Operation Order No. 1. By Lt Col J.H. Hall Commdg 16th Middx Regt.	26/06/1916	26/06/1916
Miscellaneous	Appendix A		
Miscellaneous			
Heading	29th Division. 86th Infantry Brigade. 16th Battalion Middlesex Regiment July 1916		
Heading	War Diary of 16th Middlesex Reg for July 1916		
War Diary		01/07/1916	30/07/1916
Heading	29th Division. 85th Infantry Brigade 16th Battalion Middlesex Regiment August 1916		
Heading	War Diary of 16th Middlesex Regt from 1-8-16 to 31-8-16 Volume 10		
War Diary		09/08/1916	30/08/1916
Heading	29th Division. 86th Infantry Brigade. 16th Battalion Middlesex Regiment September 1916		
Heading	War Diary of 16th Middlesex Regt From 1-9-16 to 30-9-16 Volume 11		
War Diary		09/11/1916	29/11/1916
Heading	29th Division. 86th Infantry Brigade. 16th Battalion Middlesex Regiment October 1916		
Heading	War Diary 16th Middlesex Regt 86th Brigade For The Month of October 1916 Volume 12		
War Diary		03/10/1916	31/10/1916
Heading	29th Division. 86th Infantry Brigade. 16th Battalion Middlesex Regiment November 1916		
Heading	War Diary of 16th Middlesex Regt from 1-11-16 to 30-11-16 Volume XIII		
War Diary		16/11/1916	27/11/1916
Heading	29th Division. 86th Infantry Brigade. 16th Battalion Middlesex Regiment December 1916		
Heading	War Diary of 16th Middlesex Regt From 1-12-16 to 31-12-16 Volume XIV		
War Diary		01/12/1916	14/12/1916
Heading	War Diary of 16th Middlesex Regt From 1-1-17 to 31-1-17 Volume XV		
War Diary		01/01/1917	30/01/1917

Heading	War Diary of 16th Middlesex Regt From 1-2-17 to 28-2-17 Volume XVI		
War Diary		02/02/1917	28/02/1917
Heading	War Diary 16th Middlesex Regt for the month of March 1917 Volume XVII		
War Diary		01/03/1917	30/03/1917
Heading	War Diary of 16th Middlesex Regt From 1-4-17 to 30-4-17 Volume XVIII		
War Diary		01/04/1917	27/04/1917
Heading	War Diary of 16th Battalion Middlesex Regiment From May 1st 1917 To May 31st 1917 Volume XIX		
War Diary		01/05/1917	31/05/1917
Heading	War Diary of 16th Middlesex Regt from 1-6-17 to 30-6-17 Volume XX		
War Diary		02/06/1917	27/06/1917
Heading	War Diary of 16th Middlesex Regt From July 1st 1917 to July 31st 1917 Volume XXI		
War Diary		05/07/1917	30/07/1917
Heading	War Diary of 16th Middlesex Regt From 1-8-17 to 31-8-17 Volume XXII		
War Diary		01/08/1917	28/08/1917
Heading	War Diary of 16th Middlesex Regt From 1-9-17 to 30-9-17 Volume XXIII		
War Diary		01/09/1917	30/09/1917
Heading	War Diary of 16th Middlesex Regt From 1-10-17 to 31-10-17 Volume XXIV		
War Diary		01/10/1917	30/11/1917
Map			
Miscellaneous	Message Form.		
Miscellaneous	Operation Orders By Lieut. Col. J. Forbes-Robertson. D.S.O., M.C. Commanding 16th. Battalion Middlesex Regiment.	19/11/1917	19/11/1917
Heading	War Diary of 16th Middlesex Regt From 1-12-17 to 31-12-17 Volume XXVI		
War Diary		01/12/1917	31/12/1917
War Diary	Renty	01/01/1918	15/01/1918
War Diary	Setques	16/01/1918	16/01/1918
War Diary	St. Jean.	17/01/1918	18/01/1918
War Diary	Wieltje	19/01/1918	22/01/1918
War Diary		23/01/1918	26/01/1918
War Diary	?tinghe	27/01/1918	31/01/1918
War Diary		01/02/1918	22/02/1918
Miscellaneous	16th Battalion The Middlesex Regiment. 29th Division.	01/02/1918	01/02/1918
Miscellaneous	16th Battalion The Middlesex Regiment. 29th Division.		

WO95/2302/2

29TH DIVISION
86TH INFY BDE

16TH BN MIDDX REGT

APR 1916-FEB 1918

From 33 DIV.
100 Bde.

DISBANDED
FEB 1918

29th Division.
86th Infantry Brigade.

16th BATTALION

MIDDLESEX REGIMENT

APRIL 1 9 1 6

1 Feb '18

Army Form C. 2118

Instructions regarding War Diaries and Intelligence Summaries are contained in F. S. Regs., Part II. and the Staff Manual respectively. Title Pages will be prepared in manuscript.

or

INTELLIGENCE SUMMARY

(Erase heading not required.)

XXIX 86/29 16 Middlesex Vol 6

Place	Date	Hour	Summary of Events and Information	Remarks and references to Appendices
	April. 1916 24		Battalion marches from QUIESTEDE to AIRE, entrains at AIRE and proceeds by rail to DOULLENS arriving 3.20 pm.	a.g.g.
		5pm	Battalion marches to MAILLY-MAILLET map 57D square Q 7 arriving 12.30 am. 25th	
	25		Battalion took over trenches AUCHENVILLERS section, left sector from composite unit of 1 coy 1st Lancashire Fusiliers and one coy 1st Dublin Fusiliers. relief complete 10.30 pm.	a.g.g.
	26		Casualties 1 O.R. killed.	a.g.g.
	27		do 1 O.R. killed	a.g.g.
	28		do 3 O.R. wounded.	a.g.g.
		11pm	Battalion relieved by 1st K.O.S. Borderers. and marches to ACHEUX, map 57D square P 14 arriving about 2 am. 29th. One man accidentally killed on the road at about 1 am	
	May 8	7.30pm	Battalion marches to MAILLY-MAILLET Map 57 D square Q 7 arriving about 8.30 pm	J.
	18		Battalion took over trenches AUCHONVILLERS sector from 1st Lancashire Fusiliers	J.

C. A. Jones Major for Lt Col

Comm. 16th Middlesex.

29th Division.
86th Infantry Brigade.

16th BATTALION

MIDDLESEX REGIMENT

M A Y 1 9 1 6

WAR DIARY
~~or~~
~~INTELLIGENCE SUMMARY~~
(Erase heading not required.)

Army Form C. 2118

16 Middlesex

XXIX

Vol 7

Instructions regarding War Diaries and Intelligence Summaries are contained in F. S. Regs., Part II. and the Staff Manual respectively. Title Pages will be prepared in manuscript.

Place	Date	Hour	Summary of Events and Information	Remarks and references to Appendices
	May 8		Battalion marches to MAILLY-MAILLET Map 57D square Q7 arriving about 8.30 p.m	H.
	18		Battalion took over trenches AUCHONVILLERS sector from 1st Lancashire Fusiliers	H.
	26		Casualties 1 O.R. killed, 2 O.R. wounded, 1 O.R. shell shock - in action	H.
	28		Battalion relieved by 4th Worcesters and marched to LOUVENCOURT arriving about 10.0 p.m	H.

J. Hamilton Hall Lt Col
Commanding, 16th Middlesex

1875 W. W593/826 1,000,000 4/15 J.B.C. & A.

29th Division.
86th Infantry Brigade.

16th BATTALION

MIDDLESEX REGIMENT

J U N E 1 9 1 6

Instructions regarding War Diaries and Intelligence Summaries are contained in F. S. Regs., Part II. and the Staff Manual respectively. Title Pages will be prepared in manuscript.

WAR DIARY
or
~~INTELLIGENCE SUMMARY~~
(Erase heading not required.)

16 Middlesex
29th Division
VIII Corps.

Army Form C. 2118

Page 13

Original

Vol 8

Place	Date	Hour	Summary of Events and Information	Remarks and references to Appendices
	June	1916		
	7		Battalion to MAILLY-MAILLET.	agg.
	11		Battalion to MAILLY WOOD Map 57D square P18.	agg.
	15		Battalion took over trenches in AUCHENVILLERS northern sector relieving 1st Lancashire Fusiliers. 2 officers 25 O.R. detached from battalion to join a brigade bombing company.	agg.
	21		Casualties 2 O.R. wounded.	
	23		Battalion relieved by two companies of 1st Lancs. Fusiliers, and marched to ACHEUX WOOD square P8d.	agg.
	24.		Artillery bombardment commence.	
	27		Battalion orders issued for a general assault on enemy's trenches, see Appendix I	
	Night 27/28		Lt Cleghorn and 12 O.R. carried out a raid on the enemy's trenches. At 11.10 p.m. the party left our trenches at Q 3 d 7.3. After getting through our own wire the party moved along NEW BEAUMONT ROAD up to the enemy's trenches unobserved. They found the enemy's wire considerably damaged but with no clear passages through it. This held the party up and only the officer and two men actually got through and entered the German trenches. At this moment the enemy began throwing bombs into their front trench from both flanks, and into their wire. They also opened up a heavy machine gun fire, and made a barrage of shrapnel on our front line and on the sunken road in Q 4 c. The officer gave the word to withdraw and the party returned to our own trenches. Casualties 2 O.R. wounded.	agg. agg.
	28		Orders received postponing the general assault from June 29th to July 1st	agg.
	29		1 O.R. killed 3 O.R. wounded all accidentally. These belonged to the detachment sent to the brigade bombing company.	
	30.		Reserve of 9 officers 79 O.R. drawn from the battalion and proceeded at ~~10~~ 2.30 p.m. under Major A.N.G. Jones to MAILLY WOOD. Battalion less reserve and bombing detachment) ~~and~~ strength 22 officers 689 O.R. marched to AUCHENVILLERS 10.20 pm. and bivouaced there for the night.	

1875 Wt. W593/826 1,000,000 4/15 J.B.C. & A. A.D.S.S./Forms/C. 2118.

J Hamilton Hall Lt Col
Commdg 16th Middlesex Regt

Appendix I

Copy No 10

SECRET

Ref. French Maps
BEAUMONT 57D SE (Edition 2B)
Scale 1/10000

Operation Orders No 1
by Lt Col J H Hall Commdg 16 [illegible] Regt

21 June 1916

I Own Troops (a) The British forces are to advance from the trenches to the assault on [illegible]
(b) Boundary assigned to 86th Inf Bde
North — Point (27) (Q5 c 2.8.) - Points (59) (88) (04) (all incl) to Q 12 b 70.50.
South — Point (89) (Q10 d 55 70) - Y Ravine (excl) - point (41) (Q6.c.4.1)(incl.).
(c) Allotment positions in our trenches:-
2nd RF - front line from South boundary to BRIDGE END (excl)
1st L.F. - front line from BRIDGE END (incl) to North Boundary.
1st RDF — ESSEX STREET & 88th Trenches. 16th Mx — CRIPPS CUT & CARDIFF STREET
(d) Two Stokes guns & 2 sections 1/2 Monmouthshire Regt will be attached to the battalion.
(e) The 87th Inf Bde attack on the right of 86th Inf Bde, the 4th Division attack on the left of the 86th Inf Bde, the 1st Hants Regt being on their extreme right.

II Objectives. (a) 2nd RF — 1st line system German trenches as far east as STATION ROAD; from our South boundary to line drawn from sap 100x from HAWTHORN REDOUBT to the RUIN inclusive, back to STATION ROAD.
(b) 1st LF — 1st line system German trenches, including BEAUMONT HAMEL as far East as WAGON ROAD; from left 2nd RF to our northern boundary.
(c) 1st RDF — 2nd line system German trenches BEAUCOURT ROAD, from our South boundary to point Q8 (incl).
(d) 16 Mx — 2nd line system German trenches East of BEAUCOURT ROAD from Q6 c 70.30 to Q 12 b 00.25.
(e) The 1st RDF & 16th Mx will avoid the village of BEAUMONT HAMEL as much as possible in their advance.

III Plan (a) The attack will be preceded for some days by a continuous bombardment; & the discharge of gas at certain periods. The actual time for the assault, called 0.0 in these orders will be notified later. The mine under HAWTHORN REDOUBT will be fired at -0.10 All dugouts will be vacated by -0.45.
(b) Distribution of the Battalion in our trenches on the morning of the assault:-
CRIPPS CUT — C Coy on right Bn HQ in centre, D Coy on left. C & D Coys will each have one Stokes gun with them.
CARDIFF STREET — A Coy right B Coy on left, with 2 sections 1/2 Monmouthshire Regt on right of A Coy
1st Aid Post will be in 2nd Avenue at Q Q b 95.45.
Coys will occupy a frontage of 150 yds
(c) Each Company will advance on a frontage of 100 yds. C (right) D (left) Coys leading, A Coy behind & to the right of C Coy, B Coy following A. Coys will move in platoon columns sections moving in single file & extending when necessary. Interval between sections 30 yds distance between lines 50 yds. Hd Qrs & the 2 sections Monmouth Regt will follow in A section behind B Coy.
Communication trenches to be used. [illegible] STREET with HAPPY ALLEY right of C.A.
B Coy & 2 secs Monmouth Regt, HESTON ROAD with McLAREN LANE left of C A,
B Coy & 2 secs Bn HQrs, HOUNSLOW ROAD right of D & LANSDOWNE LANE left of D.
Left flank sections of D & right flank of C.A & B. [illegible] to be [illegible] 20 yds distance.
One Stokes Gun will follow behind the right of C & D Coys; five men with [illegible] detailed will accompany each gun to carry ammunition & wear the letter "C" in white on the left arm: OC B Coy will detail the last section of each of the two platoons proceeding via HAPPY ALLEY to pick up extra ammunition en route for these two Stokes guns & dump it at STATION ROAD at Q 11 b 02.42
- Platoon Scouts (3) will move on front & exposed flanks.
- Platoon grenadiers (5) & Lewis guns will move immediately in rear of the second or third section of their platoons
Trench bridges are allotted as follows; 5 with A, 2 with C.
Bangalore Torpedoes are allotted as follows: 2 with A, 2 with C.

(d) Our front-line trenches will be crossed by the leading Cos as soon as the last wave of the 2nd RF has reached the front line of the German trenches, approximately at 0.2. Advance will be at a rate not exceeding 50 yds a minute. The advance is preceded by a barrage from our Divisional Art. which lifts 100 yds every two minutes, until they reach a line 400x East of Station + Wagon Roads where the barrage remains till 1.5.
The first objective for the Battalion will be STATION ROAD, D Coy from Q.11.a.70.70 to point 66 (excl) direction 110° & 115° magnetic for left + right of Coy respectively; C Coy from point 90 (incl) to Q11 b 02.42 (incl) direction [illegible] 109° magnetic for left + right of Coy ~~respectively~~; A Coy from left of C Coy to Q11 b 10.23, direction 115° magnetic for both left + right of Coy. B Coy will remain behind A, same line of direction, B HQ will move as soon as possible to Q11 b 02.42, the 2 sections 1/2 Monmouths Rgt remaining behind B.

(e) On arriving at STATION ROAD. (1) D Coy will immediately push on + with 2 platoons seize the S end of trench running northward from Q.11.b 00.70 (sending bombers to Q5c 85.18) + also with 2 platoons seize the N portion of new trench which runs from Q11 a 90.70 to Q11 b 20.40. It should be noted that the post 1st Hants Regt (4th Div) on our left are due to seize point 66 at 0.35 + consolidate this point with the aid of a Stokes mortar. (2) C Coy at the same time pushing on + seizing the remaining portion of this new trench sending bombers to the Southern end, + up BEAUMONT ALLEY whilst reorganizing for a further advance. (3) The Stokes gun with D + C Coys will play on the trenches in advance of the bombers proceeding up trenches to Q5c 85.18 + up BEAUMONT ALLEY. (4) A Coy will reorganize into two lines about 50 yds distance + 100 yds frontage, front line along STATION ROAD, left clear of BEAUMONT ALLEY. (5) B Coy will form up similarly, 50 yds behind A, + conform to the new direction. (6) All coys will send out Scouts to front + flanks.

(f) At 1.00 the further advance from the neighbourhood of STATION ROAD will begin:–
(1) C Coy will lead moving on a 50 yds frontage in 8 lines with 2 sections in each line, along the northern side of BEAUMONT ALLEY to point 82 then with right directed on point 41. If necessary the first two lines will be thickened after leaving point 82 to four sections each. On arrival at point 41 C Coy will send bombers up towards point 53 care being taken not to bomb into party of 1st Hants Rgt who are due to arrive at point 53 at 0.45 + bomb down towards point 41. Both Stokes Mortars will accompany C Coy, immediately behind their second line, to direct their fire onto point 41 + immediately to the right of it.
(2) A Coy will advance echeloned 100 yds behind leading line of C Coy, frontage 100 yds, four lines, direction 80° magnetic, left on point 41; if necessary on arriving within 200 yds of point 41, the Coy will advance in 2 lines. On arrival at this trench A Coy will send bombers down towards point 98 + join up with the 1st RDF who are due at point 98 at the same time.
(3) B Coy will follow A in 4 lines 50 yds distance.
(4) The 1/2 2 sections 1/2 Monmouth Rgt will follow B Coy, 100 yds distance.
(5) The 2 platoons of D Coy in new trench at Q11 a 90.70 with one Lewis gun will follow C Coy along BEAUMONT ALLEY, bombing any dugouts passed over by C Coy, the last two sections picking up prisoners &c. The two platoons of D Coy with 1 Lewis gun in trench running Northward from Q11 b 00 70 will continue to protect the left flank of the battalion from [illegible] which might be directed from that trench. These platoons will join at point 41 after the arrival of the battalion at its final objective.
(6) Bn HQ will follow behind the two platoons of D Coy working up BEAUMONT ALLEY to point 82 thence on to point 41.
(7) The Artillery barrage which remains 400 yds East of WAGON + STATION ROADS till 1.15 lifts at that time by 100 yds every 2 mins, till it reaches the trenches at BEAUCOURT RIDGE where it remains till 1.20.

(g). If serious opposition is met with at trench (41) Coys will reorganise there before pushing on to their final objective, otherwise they will push on immediately, leaving the clearing up here to be done by the last line of sections of B Coy + D Coy. The two Stokes guns will as soon as possible open fire on the centre portion of the new trench forming the final objective.

(h) With the exception of last part of (g) Coys must push on till they reach their final objective, where they will consolidate: communication trenches will not be used, troops must move over the open ground. On no account are troops to stop because formations on their flanks are held up. Experience has proved that the best way to assist troops who are being held up, is to push forward & to outflank the enemy.

(i) On arrival at the final objective, A + C will send bombing parties down & up the trench respectively, & A, B & C Coys will send out covering parties to the front (& flanks if necessary) whilst consolidation is immediately taken in hand on the following general line:-

(1) Front line from Q11 b 00.85 to Q6 c 90.34; Cos 80 yds each, A on right, B in centre, C on left.

(2) Second line from Q12 a 30.95 to Q6 b 70.30. Cos 80 yds each, A on right, B in centre, C on left.

(3) D Coy circular line from Q12 a 55 95 to Q6 c 58 14 to Q6 c 45 16

(4) 2 Sections 1/2 Monmouthshire Regt from Q12 a 55 95 to point 41 to Q6 c 45.16.

IV Communications (a) With Bn HQ there will be 13 Signallers, divided into two parties, one party to communicate with Bde HQ + Cos + one party to communicate with Aeroplanes. These will be supplemented by six Runners.

(b) With each Coy there will be 4 signallers (with a reserve of 4 signallers in the last line of sections of each Coy) divided into two parties, one party to communicate with Bn HQ + one party to communicate with Aeroplanes. These will be supplemented by six Runners. One of the 4 signallers will be supplied from the service section.

(c) As Bn HQ will move forward in two sections, the party enumerated in (a) will be further subdivided into two parties.

(d) If heavy artillery fire is required on any particular locality the prefix HA followed by the map square designation of the target will be sent.

(e) Two aeroplanes are being employed continuously as contact patrols.

V Medical Coy stretcher bearers will in the first instance remain behind & clear the trenches of any wounded, reporting to the Bn MO at the First Aid Post. The MO & First Aid Post will move forward as soon as possible on the same line as Bn HQ. Advanced dressing stations are established at TENDERLOIN & MICHONVILLERS.

VI. Discipline (a) Our own wounded must be left alone by our men. On no account are men to fall out to attend to them.

(b) No looting is allowed. This is a Court Martial Offence for which the punishment is "to be shot"

VII Equipment &c The details of equipment, ammunition &c, to be carried is shown in Appendix A. All ranks will wear the Divisional Badge, tin triangle & Flash bag. Bombers will have a red patch painted on top of their Steel helmets. Bombing parties will carry the special flags to denote their presence in the trenches; they must never be planted in the ground.

VIII. Reinforcements Officers in excess of 5 per Coy & 10% of other ranks will remain behind in 60th Trench under the 2nd in Command till sent forward. The detail of those composing this party has been issued separately.

Appendix A

Packs 1. All [illegible]
the Q.M. [illegible]

[illegible] (a) All [illegible]

[illegible] S.A.A. each. 2000 rounds S.A.A. will be carried [illegible] gun

(d) Signallers; carry 120 rounds S.A.A. no pick or shovel.

(e) [illegible] may be [illegible] 120 rounds S.A.A. no [illegible]

(f) [illegible]

(g) [illegible] Platoon [illegible] these [illegible] must be taken by other men.

(h) [illegible]

(i) [illegible]

(j) [illegible]

3. All [illegible]

IX Trench Traffic. Trenches will be reserved as follows:-
Up traffic - TIPPERARY & 2nd AVENUE
Down " - BROADWAY & 3rd AVENUE

X 1st Line Transport. Limbers & Water Carts should be prepared to join the battalion at dusk on Z day

XI Maps, Papers. The only maps to be referred to in all messages & to be carried in the attack are the 1/10000 BEAUMONT TRENCH MAP Sheet 57D SE & 1/20000 Sheet 57D SE. NO other maps will be carried by Officers or men. Officers & NCOs will carry notebooks, but no other papers will be taken.

XII Watches. Watches will be synchronised daily at 9.30am & 7.30 pm by the Adjutant on X & Y days.

XIII Reports. 16th HQ will be in the centre of CRIPPS CUT on assembly; it moves to S W end of BEAUMONT ALLEY in rear of B Coy., & follows the final advance to point (82) thence to point (41) when it will be established: reports to be rendered accordingly.

Capt & Adjt
16th Middx Regt

Copy No 1 OC A
2 B
3 C
4 D
5 C.O.
6 2nd C.O.
7 HQ
8 86th Inf Bde
9 1st Hants
10 War Diary.

29th Division.

86th Infantry Brigade.

16th BATTALION

MIDDLESEX REGIMENT

J U L Y 1 9 1 6

86/29

War Diary

of

16th Middlesex Regt

for

July 1916

86/9

Instructions regarding War Diaries and Intelligence Summaries are contained in F. S. Regs., Part II. and the Staff Manual respectively. Title pages will be prepared in manuscript.

WAR DIARY
or
~~INTELLIGENCE SUMMARY.~~
(Erase heading not required.)

Army Form C. 2118.

16th Middlesex Regt.
29th Division,
VIII Corps.

Page 14

Vol 9

Place	Date	Hour	Summary of Events and Information	Remarks and references to Appendices
	July 1916			
	1		Battalion in action 7.30 a.m. from support trenches.	
			Casualties Officers Killed 3 Wounded 10 Missing believed killed 6 Missing 5	
			O.R " 19 306 37 138	
		10.15 am	Balance of Battalion took over front line trenches AUCHONVILLERS Sector.	
	3	noon	Battalion relieved in front line trenches by 1st R.D.Fusiliers; 2 Coys remaining in 88th Trench, 2 Coys + Batt HQ proceeding to AUCHONVILLERS	
	4	5.30 pm	Battalion moves to billets in ENGLEBELMER, being in Brigade Reserve. Some shelling of billets during night + periodically during next few days.	
	8		Battalion takes over trenches ENGLEBELMER Sector (KNIGHTSBRIDGE) from 2nd Hants Regt & South Wales Borderers. Relief completed by 7.0 pm. Casualties, O.R. Wounded 3	
	12		Casualties, O.R. Wounded 1	
	13		Casualties O.R. Killed 1, Wounded 1.	
	15		Battalion relieved by 1st R.D.F. + moves to billets in ENGLEBELMER: periodical shelling of this village took place during period 15th to 23rd inst.	
	18		Reinforcements 134 other ranks arrived about 9.30 pm	
	19		Casualties O.R. Wounded 1. (shell shock)	
			" " " 1.	
	23	2.0 pm	Battalion marches from ENGLEBELMER to WARNIMONT WOOD, proceeding via BERTRANCOURT + BUS-LES-ARTOIS, on Brigade being relieved from duty in front line trenches.	
			Reinforcements 1 Captain, 10 second Lieutenants, arrived about 10 pm.	
	24	8.45 am	Brigade marches to BEAUVAL proceeding via AUTHIE, MARIEUX + BEAUQUESNE.	
	27	1.45 pm	Battalion marches from BEAUVAL to DOULLENS, entrains + proceeds to ESQUELBECQ arriving 10 pm, then marching to WORMHOUDT, arriving about 1.0 am 28th inst.	
	30	7.30 am	Battalion entrains at WORMHOUDT for POPERINGHE arriving 9.0 a.m. transport proceeding by road	
			Battalion in Camp C in wood, 3 miles East of POPERINGHE, Map 28 Square A 30.	

J. Hamilton Hall
Lt Col
Comdg 16th Middx Regt

3353 Wt. W2544/1454 700,000 5/15 D. D. & L. A.D.S.S./Forms/C. 2118.

29th Division.

86th Infantry Brigde

16th BATTALION

MIDDLESEX REGIMENT

AUGUST 1 9 1 6

Confidential

War Diary

of

16th Middlesex Regt

From 1-8-16 to 31-8-16.

(Volume 10)

Army Form C. 2118

WAR DIARY
or
~~INTELLIGENCE SUMMARY~~
(Erase heading not required.)

Instructions regarding War Diaries and Intelligence Summaries are contained in F. S. Regs., Part II. and the Staff Manual respectively. Title Pages will be prepared in manuscript.

16th Middlesex Regt
29th Division,
VIII Corps.

Vol. 10.
Page 15

Place	Date	Hour	Summary of Events and Information	Remarks and references to Appendices
	Aug 1916			
	9	9.30pm	Bn entrains for YPRES, becoming in Brigade Reserve; & billeted in dugouts on Canal Bank, Map 28, square I.1.b.	
	11		Casualties, 4 O.R. wounded	
	12		" 1 OR. Killed, 1 OR. wounded	
	18	9.0pm	Bn moves off for trenches, relieving 1st Essex Regt in POTIJZE Sector, Bn Hd Qrs in Chateau Grounds Potijze, Map 28, square I.4.a.	
	23		Casualties. 1 OR. wounded	
	29		" 1 OR Killed. 1 wounded.	
	29/30		Bn is relieved by 1st Essex Regt, and marches to YPRES, being in Brigade Reserve	
	30	9.30pm	On being relieved by 2nd Hants Regt, Bn proceeds to Camp C Map 28 square A30.	

J. Hamilton Hall .... LT. COLONEL,
COMMNDG. 16th SERVICE BATTALION
MIDDLESEX REGIMENT.

1875 Wt. W593/826 1,000,000 4/15 J.B.C. & A. A.D.S.S./Forms/C. 2118.

29th Division.
86th Infantry Brigade.

16th BATTALION

MIDDLESEX REGIMENT

SEPTEMBER 1 9 1 6

1632
8B

Vol XI

Confidential

War Diary
of
16th Middlesex Regt
From 1-9-16 to 30-9-16.
(Volume 11)

✕

WAR DIARY
or
~~INTELLIGENCE SUMMARY.~~
(Erase heading not required.)

Army Form C. 2118.

Instructions regarding War Diaries and Intelligence Summaries are contained in F. S. Regs., Part II. and the Staff Manual respectively. Title pages will be prepared in manuscript.

16th Middlesex Regt
29th Division
VIII Corps.

Vol 11
Page 16

Place	Date	Hour	Summary of Events and Information	Remarks and references to Appendices
September 1916				
	9	8.45pm	Bn entrains for YPRES, becoming in Brigade Reserve, billeted in dugouts on Canal Bank, Map 28 Square I.1.b	
	11		Casualties O.R. Wounded 1.	
	12		" " Killed 1.	
	14	8.0pm	Bn moves off for Trenches, relieving 1st Royal Dublin Fusiliers in WEILTJE Sector, Bn HQrs St JEAN Map 28 square C.27.b	
	15		Casualties O.R. Killed, 1, Wounded 2.	
	16		" " Wounded 1.	
	17		" " " 2.	
	19/20		Bn is relieved by 2nd South Wales Borderers, & marches to YPRES, becoming in Brigade Reserve.	
	23		Bn moves off to trenches relieving 1st Royal Dublin Fusiliers in POTIJZE Sector. Bn HQ in Chateau Grounds, Map 28 sq. I.4.a	
	27		Casualties OR Killed 1, Wounded 2.	
	"		Officers Wounded 1	
	28		Bn is relieved by 2nd Hampshire Rgt & marches to YPRES, becoming in Brigade Res.	
	29	8.0pm	On being relieved by 1st Essex Regt, Bn entrains for BRANDHOEK & proceeds to Camp C, Map 28. square A30.	

F R Hill
Major, for
Lt Col, Commdg 16 Middlesex Rgt

2353 Wt. W2544/1454 700,000 5/15 D. D. & L. A.D.S.S./Forms/C. 2118.

29th Division.
86th Infantry Brigade.

16th BATTALION

MIDDLESEX REGIMENT

OCTOBER 1 9 1 6

Vol 12

Confidential

165/2
86B

War Diary

16th Middlesex Regt.

86th Brigade

for the month of

October 1916

Volume 12.

Instructions regarding War Diaries and Intelligence Summaries are contained in F. S. Regs., Part II. and the Staff Manual respectively. Title pages will be prepared in manuscript.

WAR DIARY
or
~~INTELLIGENCE SUMMARY~~
(Erase heading not required.)

16th Middlesex Regt
29th Division.

Army Form C. 2118.

Vol 12
Page 17

Place	Date	Hour	Summary of Events and Information	Remarks and references to Appendices
	October 1916			
16th	3.	1.0 pm	Battn marches to POPERINGHE & entrains for WORMHOUDT, Map 27 sq. O 16.	
	8	7.30 am	Battn entrains for POPERINGHE, thence entraining for LONGUEAU, AMIENS.	
	9	2.0 am	Battn detrains, & marches to LA NEUVILLE arriving 9.0 a.m.	
	10		Battn marches to DERNANCOURT, Map: ALBERT, Sq. E 21.	
	13		Battn moves off from DERNANCOURT, and is bivouacked S E of MAMETZ WOOD, Map. ALBERT Sq S. 20.c.	
	19.		Battn relieves Berkshire Regt in Right Subsector of Left Sector (FLERS), Bn HQ at N 31 b 5.0. ALBERT Combined Sheet.	
	20.		Casualties: O.R. 5 K. 9 W.	
	21		" Officers W. 1. O.R. - 5 "	
	22		" - 4 " 14 " 1 M.	
	23		" Officers M. 1. O.R. 8 K. 22 W.	
	.		On being relieved by 1st Lancashire Fusiliers, Battn is in reserve in SWITCH TRENCH, S.E. of FLERS. Heavy shelling periodically during next 2 days	
	25		Casualties O.R. Killed 2.	
	25		Battn relieves 1st Lancashire Fusiliers in the line, 1 company being accommodated in trenches S of DELVILLE WOOD.	
	26		Casualties. Officers. W. 1. O.R. W 3.	
	27		" O.R. K. 3 - W 6.	
	"		On being relieved by 1st Essex Regt, Battn moves to bivouac in TRONES WOOD, 2 Cos. being left in SWITCH TRENCH	
	29		Battn marches to billets in ALBERT.	
	31		Battn marches to CORBIE,	

J. Hamilton Hall Lt. Col.
Comndt. 16 Middlesex R.

29th Division.

86th Infantry Brigade.

16th BATTALION

MIDDLESEX REGIMENT

NOVEMBER 1 9 1 6

16/R

SB

Vol 13

Confidential.

War Diary

of

16th Middlesex Regt.

From 1-11-16. to 30-11-16.

(Volume XIII)

Instructions regarding War Diaries and Intelligence Summaries are contained in F. S. Regs., Part II. and the Staff Manual respectively. Title pages will be prepared in manuscript.

WAR DIARY
or
~~INTELLIGENCE SUMMARY.~~
(Erase heading not required.)

Army Form C.2118.

16th Middlesex Regt.
29th Division.

Vol XIII
Page 18.

Place	Date	Hour	Summary of Events and Information	Remarks and references to Appendices
16th Mx	November 1916.			
	16.		Battalion marches to MEAULTE. Map. ALBERT Combined Sheet, E.17.	
	18		Battalion marches to CARNOY, being in reserve in Camp, at A.8.	
	21		Battalion marches to GUILLEMONT, T.19.	
	23		Battalion relieves 1st Royal Inniskilling Fusiliers in trenches LESBOEUFS.	
	23		Casualties. Other Ranks, Killed 2, Wounded 2.	
	24		" " " 1 " 5	
	25		" " " 3 " 12	
	26		" " " 1 " 4	
	26		Battalion is relieved by 1st K.O.S.B's & marches to GUILLEMONT.	
	27		Battalion marches to CARNOY & becomes in reserve in Camp at A8.	

J. Hamilton Hall Lt Col
Commdg: 16th Middlesex Regt.

2353 Wt. W2544/1454 700,000 5/15 D. D. & L. A.D.S.S./Forms/C. 2118.

29th Division.
86th Infantry Brigde

))-------

;6th BATTALION

MIDDLESEX REGIMENT

DECEMBER 1 9 1 6

Vol 14

16/12
8/B

<u>Confidential.</u>

War Diary

of

16th Middlesex Regt

From 1-12-16 to 31-12-16.

(Volume XIV)

Instructions regarding War Diaries and Intelligence Summaries are contained in F. S. Regs., Part II. and the Staff Manual respectively. Title pages will be prepared in manuscript.

WAR DIARY
or
~~INTELLIGENCE SUMMARY.~~
(Erase heading not required.)

16th Middlesex Regt.
29th Division.
XIV. Corps.

Army Form C. 2118.
Vol XIV
Page 19.

Place	Date	Hour	Summary of Events and Information	Remarks and references to Appendices
	December 1916.			
	1st		Battalion marches to GUILLEMONT, becoming in Brigade reserve.	
	2nd		Battalion takes over trenches, LES BOEUFS.	
	3rd		Casualties;- Other Ranks - Killed 2	
	4th		" 4	
	5th		On being relieved by 1st Royal Inniskilling Fus, Battalion marches to GUILLEMONT	
	6th		Battalion proceeds to MANSEL CAMP (Near MAMETZ)	
	8th		Battalion marches to GUILLEMONT	
	9th		Battalion relieves 1st Lancs Fus in line, MORVAL.	
	10th		Casualties; other ranks - Killed 1, wounded 6.	
	"		Battalion is relieved and marches to CARNOY	
	11th		Battalion marches to MEAULTE.	
	14th		Battalion entrains at EDGE HILL, (DERNANCOURT), for LONGPRÉ, and marches to BREILLY, 10 Kilometres, N.W of AMIENS., arriving about 2-30 a.m 15th.	

[illegible signature] Major, for
Lieut Colonel,
Commdg 16th Middlesex Rgt.

86/39

Vol 15

Confidential

War Diary
of
16th Middlesex Regt
From 1-1-17 to 31-1-17.
(Volume XV)

Instructions regarding War Diaries and Intelligence Summaries are contained in F. S. Regs., Part II. and the Staff Manual respectively. Title pages will be prepared in manuscript.

WAR DIARY
or
~~INTELLIGENCE SUMMARY.~~
(*Erase heading not required.*)

16th Middlesex Regt
29th Division
XIV Corps.

Army Form C. 2118.

Vol XV
Page 20

Place	Date	Hour	Summary of Events and Information	Remarks and references to Appendices
January 1917				
	9th	3.0pm	Battalion leaves BREILLY and marches to St PIERRE-A-GUOY en route for entraining Station for forward area.	
	10th	4.15am	Battalion moves off for HANGEST, and entrains for CORBIE, arriving 10 am.	
	11th	11 am	Battalion marches to VILLE-SUR-ANCRE	
	14th	10 am	Battalion marches to CARNOY, Camp 3. - A8a. - on CARNOY-MONTAUBAN Road	
	15th	2.30p	Battalion marches to GUILLEMONT	
	16th		Battalion takes over the line from 1st R. Dublin Fusiliers in MORVAL Sector. Bn HQ. T.12.A.6.8.	
	18		Battalion is relieved by 4th Worcestershire Regt; and marches to Camp 3 CARNOY.	
	21		Battalion marches to GUILLEMONT	
	22		Battalion relieves 1st Royal Dublin Fusiliers in the line.	
	24		Battalion is relieved by 4th Worcestershire Regt & marches to camp 3 CARNOY	
	27		Battalion marches from CARNOY to GUILLEMONT.	
	28		Battalion relieves 1st Royal Dublin Fusiliers in the line. Casualties 3 OR wounded 1 Death from exposure	
	30		Battalion is relieved by 4th Worcestershire Regt and marches to Camp 3 CARNOY.	

J. Hamilton Hall Lt Col
Commdg 16th Middlesex Regt.

2353 Wt. W2544/1454 700,000 5/15 D. D. & L. A.D.S.S./Forms/C. 2118.

Vol 16

86/29

Confidential

War Diary
of
16th Middlesex Regt.
from 1-2-17 to 28-2-17.

(Volume XVI)

Instructions regarding War Diaries and Intelligence Summaries are contained in F. S. Regs., Part II. and the Staff Manual respectively. Title pages will be prepared in manuscript.

WAR DIARY
or
INTELLIGENCE SUMMARY.
(Erase heading not required.)

16th Middlesex Regt
29th Division
XIV Corps

Army Form C. 2118.

Vol XVI
Page 21

Place	Date	Hour	Summary of Events and Information	Remarks and references to Appendices
	2/2/17		Battalion to GUILLEMONT.	
	3/2/17		Battalion took over MORVAL SECTOR from 1st Royal Dublin Fusiliers. Batn HQ T.12.A.6.8. Map 57C. Edition 1.	
	5/2/17		Battalion is relieved by 4th Worcestershire Regt, and marches to CARNOY.	
	7/2/17		Battalion proceeds by bus to BUSSY-LES-DAOURS, and becomes in Corps Reserve	
	7-20/2/17		Rest & training.	
	21/2/17		Battalion marches to CORBIE and entrains for PLATEAU (A 20 A. Map 62C N.W. Edition 3A), then marching to BRONFAY CAMP 107. (L.5.A 2.8. Map 62D. N.E. Edition 2B)	
	22/2/17		Battalion marches to MALTZHORN CAMP (South of TRONES WOOD)	
	23/2/17		Battalion takes over line, SAILLY-SAILLISEL, from 1st Royal Dublin Fusiliers. Casualties: Officers, wounded 1, Others, killed 1 wounded 10.	
	25/2/17		Battalion is relieved by 2nd South Wales Borderers, and marches to COMBLES.	
	26/2/17		Battalion, less 3 officers, 120 OR, marches to BRONFAY CAMP 108.	
	28/2/17		3 Officers, 120 OR. in action as "Mopping-up" party, SAILLY-SAILLISEL. Casualties, Officer Killed 1, Wounded 1, Others Killed 3 Wounded 43, Missing 2. Remainder of Battalion BRONFAY to HARDECOURT.	

[illegible] Lt Col
Comdg 16th Middlesex Regt

Vol 17

Confidential

War Diary

16th Middlesex Regt

For the month of

March 1917

Volume XVII

Instructions regarding War Diaries and Intelligence Summaries are contained in F. S. Regs., Part II. and the Staff Manual respectively. Title pages will be prepared in manuscript.

WAR DIARY
or
~~INTELLIGENCE SUMMARY.~~
(Erase heading not required.)

16th Middlesex Regt.
29th Division.
XIV Corps.

Army Form C. 2118.

Volume XVII
Page 22.

Place	Date	Hour	Summary of Events and Information	Remarks and references to Appendices
MARCH ~~February~~ 1917.				
	1		Battalion takes over line SAILLY-SAILLISEL from ~~1st Royal Dublin Fusiliers~~ 7th Lancashire Fusiliers	
			Casualties: Offrs wounded 1. Others killed 2. wounded 4.	
	3.		Battalion is relieved by 7th Somerset L. Infty and marches to HARDECOURT.	
	4		Battalion entrains at PLATEAU & proceeds to MERICOURT L'ABBÉ.	
	5th		Battalion commences an intensive training for open warfare	
	20th		Battalion proceeds by rail from EDGEHILL (DERNANCOURT) to AIRAINES, marching to WARLUS, where training is continued.	
	29th		Battalion marches to HANGEST-SUR-SOMME	
	30		Battalion marches to HALLOY PERNOIS.	

B Thorp[illegible]
Lt Col.,
Commdg 16th Middlesex Regt

8353 Wt. W2544/1454 700,000 5/15 D. D. & L. A.D.S.S./Forms/C. 2118.

Vol 18

86/29

Confidential

War Diary

of

16th Middlesex Regt

from 1.4.17 to 30.4.17

(Volume XVIII)

Instructions regarding War Diaries and Intelligence Summaries are contained in F. S. Regs., Part II. and the Staff Manual respectively. Title pages will be prepared in manuscript.

WAR DIARY
or
~~INTELLIGENCE SUMMARY.~~
(Erase heading not required.)

16th Middlesex Regt
29th Division
XVIII Corps.

Army Form C. 2118.

Volume XVIII
Page 23.

Place	Date	Hour	Summary of Events and Information	Remarks and references to Appendices
	April 1917.			
	1		Battalion marches from HALLOY-L-PERNOIS to GÉZAINCOURT (Map LENS 11 D5)	
	2		" " to HALLOY (F.5)	
	3		" " SUS-ST LEGER (F4)	
	8		" " BAVINCOURT (G.4)	
	11		" " SIMENCOURT (H.3)	
	12		" " ARRAS.	
	13	6.0am	" to original German first line trenches near TILLOY-LEZ-MOFFLAINES.	
		8.0pm	" " " third " "	
	14	1.0pm	" to ORANGE HILL. Casualties, Other Ranks: K.7. W.10.	
	"	8.0pm	" moves off to take over front line from 2nd Hants Regt in MONCHY-LE-FREUX.	
	15–18		" engaged in making new defences of MONCHY. Casualties. Officers. K.1. W.1. others. K.7. W.59. M.3.	
	18/19		" is relieved by 2nd Royal Fusiliers & 1st Royal Dublin Fusiliers, and marches to ARRAS, being billeted in chalk mine, RONVILLE.	
	21	6.0pm	Bn moves forward and takes over line from 2nd Royal Fusiliers.	
	22		Hostile aeroplane brought down by our L Gun fire.	
	22/23		Bn is relieved by 1st KOSB's & 1st R.I.F., and marches to position between ORANGE HILL and MONCHY.	
	23	noon	Bn comes under orders of G.O.C. 88th Brigade, and during the day the disposition becomes as follows:- H.Q. N.12.A.5.3: B Coy in SPRING, PICK, and SHOVEL TRENCHES; A Coy Strong Points O.7.B.6.3 to O.8.A.0.7 D Coy Southern end of SHRAPNEL TRENCH. C Coy, 2 Platoons, O.8.B.0.2 to trench South of that point. C Coy, 2 platoons, O.7.B.8.6.	
			B.Coy brings heavy Lewis Gun fire on Hostile counter attack on Copse at O.8.B.0.2.	
		6 pm	Battalion again comes under orders of G.O.C 86th Inf Bde.	
	23/24		Battalion is ordered to take over SHRAPNEL TRENCH, O.2.C.2.0 to O.2.A.3.2. Owing to the few remaining hours of darkness this was not done.	
	24/25		Bn is relieved by 2 Coys of 2nd Suffolk Regt, and marches to ARRAS, being billeted in GRAND PLACE. Casualties during period 21–25/4/17. Officers W 6. Others K.13. W75. Missing 10.	
	25		Bn proceeds by bus to BERNEVILLE.	
	26		Bn marches to WANQUETIN	
	27		" " " SOUASTRE.	

[signature] Major for Lt Col
Comndg 16th Middlesex Regt

2353 Wt. W2544/1454 700,000 5/15 D. D. & L. A.D.S.S./Forms/C. 2118.

Vol 19

86/29

Confidential

War Diary

of

16th Battalion Middlesex Regiment

From May 1st 1917 - To May 31st 1917

(Volume XIX)

Instructions regarding War Diaries and Intelligence Summaries are contained in F. S. Regs., Part II. and the Staff Manual respectively. Title Pages will be prepared in manuscript.

WAR DIARY
or
~~INTELLIGENCE SUMMARY~~
(Erase heading not required.)

16th Middlesex Regt
29th Division.
VI Corps

Army Form C. 2118

Volume XIX

Page 24.

Place	Date	Hour	Summary of Events and Information	Remarks and references to Appendices
	May 1917.			
	1	6.0 am	Battalion marches from SOUASTRE to GOUY-EN-ARTOIS, Map 51C - P.18	
	2	7.30 pm	" " GOUY-EN-ARTOIS to ARRAS	
	10		Battalion is ordered to dig strong points at N.6.C (West of MONCHY-LE-PREUX) Casualties, OFFICERS, Killed 2 wounded 1. OTHERS, Killed 1, wounded 25, Missing 1.	
	11		Battalion marches from ARRAS to BERNEVILLE.	
	15		" " " BERNEVILLE to ARRAS.	
	19	9.30 pm	Battalion marches to BROWN LINE, HQ. at N.4.A., taking over from 1st K.O.S.B's.	
	20/21		" is relieved by 1st Royal Dublin Fusiliers, and takes over front line, Right Battalion Sector, from 1st Inniskilling Fusiliers. Companies in HILL, SHRAPNEL & DALE TRENCHES, HQ at O.1.C.3.5.	
	24/25		Battalion is relieved by 2nd Royal Fusiliers, and takes over MONCHY DEFENCES, HQ at O.1.C 3 9.	
	26/27		" " " by 1st Lancashire Fusiliers and marches to BROWN LINE, HQ at N.4.A.	
	28/29		" takes over part of Right Battalion Sector - 2½ Coys in HILL TRENCH, 1½ Coys in DALE TRENCH	
	30.		" 11 Officers & 230 others strong, in conjunction with 1st Lancashire Fus in centre & 8th E. Lancashires on right, attacked HOOK TRENCH under intense artillery barrage. The left failed to get in, but 2½ Companies gained the objective, some of the centre battalion also reached the objective. The battalion on the right failed to reach the objective. All were driven back by counter-attacks, with the exception, as far as can be ascertained, of 2 Officers and some 30 to 40 men of the battalion. These detachments held out until about midday on the 31st when they were compelled to give in through lack of bombs and ammunition, and no hope of any immediate relief. Casualties 19th-31st - Officers: Killed 1, Wounded, 3 Missing, 2 Missing blvd Prisoners. 2 Others: " 31 " 139 " 70 " 6.	
	31/1		Battalion is relieved by 1st KOSB's and marches to ARRAS.	

J. Walbrugg [illegible] Capt.
Commanding
16th Battalion Middlesex Regt

1875 Wt. W593/826 1,000,000 4/15 J.B.C. & A. A.D.S.S./Forms/C. 2118.

Vol 20

Confidential

War Diary

of

16th Middlesex Regt

From 1-6-17 to 30-6-17

Volume XX

Army Form C. 2118

WAR DIARY
or
~~INTELLIGENCE SUMMARY~~
(Erase heading not required.)

Instructions regarding War Diaries and Intelligence Summaries are contained in F. S. Regs., Part II. and the Staff Manual respectively. Title Pages will be prepared in manuscript.

16th Middlesex Regt
29th Division.
XIV Corps.

Volume XX Page 25.

Place	Date	Hour	Summary of Events and Information	Remarks and references to Appendices
	June 1917			
	2nd		Battalion marches from ARRAS to BERNEVILLE.	
	3rd		Battalion marches to BEAUMETZ-L-LOGES and entrains for PERNOIS, SOMME (Map, LENS 11 – C.6), for reorganization and training.	
	24th		Battalion marches from PERNOIS to CANDAS Railhead and entrains for REXPOEDE, marching thence to billets S.W of PROVEN (Map 27NE. E23)	
	27th		Battalion becomes in Divisional Reserve.	

[signature] Lt. Col.
Commdg 16th Middlesex Regt.

1875 Wt. W593/826 1,000,000 4/15 J.B.C. & A. A.D.S.S./Forms/C. 2118.

Vol 21

Confidential.

War Diary

of

16th Middlesex Regt.

From July 1st 1917 to July 31st 1917.

(Volume XXI)

WAR DIARY
or
~~INTELLIGENCE SUMMARY~~
(Erase heading not required.)

Army Form C. 2118

Instructions regarding War Diaries and Intelligence Summaries are contained in F. S. Regs., Part II. and the Staff Manual respectively. Title Pages will be prepared in manuscript.

16th Middlesex Regt.
29th Division
XIV Corps.

Volume XXI Page 26

Place	Date	Hour	Summary of Events and Information	Remarks and references to Appendices
	July 1917.			
	5th		Battalion, less A Coy, marches to camp at A.11.C. Central (Map 28).	
	6th		D Coy marches to ELVERDINGHE, B & C Coys to Supports in B.17. HQ in bivouacs at DEAD MAN'S FARM, B.17 central.	
	7th		Casualties, other ranks wounded 10.	
	10th		" " " Killed 1, wounded 7.	
	13th		" " " " 1.	
	13th		HQ, A Coy (less 1 Officer & 50 OR) B, C, & D Coys move into wood at B.23 A. 1 Officer & 50 OR. of A Coy, and details, in camp at A.9.a.5.5.	
	15th		Casualties, O.R. Killed 1, wounded 12.	
	16th		" " " 3.	
	17th		" " " 1.	
	17th		Battalion takes over front line C7 & C13 from 2nd Royal Fusiliers	
	18th		Casualties, OR wounded 1.	
	19th		" 4 Subalterns, wounded: Other ranks Killed 9, wounded 44.	
	20		" Others wounded 4.	
	20.		Battalion is relieved by 10th Welsh Regiment (38th Division) and marches to camp in Corps staging area at X 29 d 7.3, Sheet 19.	
	24		Battalion marches to P3 Area (E 5 b. 5.5; Map 27) for training purposes.	
	30	11.52 pm	Battalion marches to new camp at F3 a 6.3 (Map 27), being in Corps reserve during operations commencing 31st.	

[signature] Lt. Col
Commdg 16th Middlesex Regt.

1875 Wt. W593/826 1,000,000 4/15 J.B.C. & A. A.D.S.S./Forms/C. 2118.

Confidential

War Diary

of

16th Middlesex Regiment

From 1.8.17 to 31.8.17

Volume XXII

Vol 22

Instructions regarding War Diaries and Intelligence Summaries are contained in F. S. Regs., Part II. and the Staff Manual respectively. Title pages will be prepared in manuscript.

WAR DIARY
or
~~INTELLIGENCE~~ SUMMARY.

(Erase heading not required.)

16th Middlesex Regt
29th Division.
XIV Corps

Army Form C. 2118.

Volume XXII. Page 27

Place	Date	Hour	Summary of Events and Information	Remarks and references to Appendices
	August 1917.			
	1st		Battalion is in Camp at F3 a. 6 3 (Sheet 27).	HhJ
	6th		Battalion moves into Corps Reserve at Camp B. 7 c. and relieves 1st Royal Dublin Fusiliers.	HhJ
	7th		" " " GREEN LINE, relieving 1st Royal Dublin Fusiliers. Battn. Hd Qrs at SAULES FARM (Ref U. 25. b 4 2. LANGEMARK 1.10,000)	HhJ
	9th - 10th		" " " FRONT LINE " " " " " " " FOURCHE FARM (" U. 20 c 9 3 " ")	HhJ
	10th - 11th		"B" and "D" Coys push out Posts across STEENBEEK (Ref between U. 20. b. 8 6 and U. 21. c. 5 7. LANGEMARK 1.10,000) In touch with French on left and 1st Lancashire Fusiliers on right. Prisoners taken 22 unwounded, 3 wounded.	HhJ
	11th - 12th		"A" Coy (3 Platoons) under Capt. J.A.W. WILSON. M.C. with 2/Lieuts. MUMFORD and SIMPSON move up from Support Line and line up in three lines W. of STEENBEEK and at 4-20 am under a pocket barrage attack PASSERELLE FARM (Ref U. 21 c 3.9 LANGEMARK. 1.10,000). Attack successful - position consolidated and held. Two Machine Guns and one Howitzer captured. 3 wounded prisoners taken. Total Casualties for tour. Officers - 2/Lt Hearne Smith 2/Lt C.W. Bishop killed. 2/Lieuts. Mumford, Simpson, Lewis, Harrison wounded Other ranks - 30 killed, 83 wounded.	HhJ
	12th - 13th		Battalion is relieved by 1st Border Regt and marches back to Camp at B. 7 c + d (Sheet 28 N.W.)	HhJ
	14th		Battalion moves to CHARTERHOUSE CAMP into Divisional Reserve (A. 12 c. Sheet 28 NW). T/Lieut Col. G. G. G. Morris D.S.O. BORDER REGT. takes over command of Battalion vice A/Lieut Col. T. W. O'Reilly to Corps Depot.	HhJ
	16th	2 pm	Battalion moves to Wood 16 (U. 25. c. LANGEMARK 1.10,000) and at 8.15 pm moves up to BLUE LINE relieving Detachments of S.W.B.s K.O.S.B.s 2nd Hants and Newfoundland Regts with Posts N.W. + S.E. of MONTMIRAIL FARM, at DENAIN FARM, MARTIN HILL and RAILWAY. Battn. Hd Qrs at SENTIER FARM. (Ref. LANGEMARK 1.10,000).	HhJ
	16th - 17th		Lieut. Col. G. G. G. Morris D.S.O. killed in action. Capt. J.A.W. Wilson M.C. assumes command of the Battalion	HhJ
	17th		T/Major J. Forbes Robertson. D.S.O. M.C. Border Regt attached Newfoundland Regt takes over command of the Battalion	HhJ
	18th - 19th		Battalion relieves 1st Royal Inniskilling Fusiliers in Front Line and Support with French on left and 1st Royal Dublin Fusiliers on right (Left Battalion Sector) U. 15 Central to U. 16 c. 1.3. Battn. Hd Qrs at WIJDENDRIFT BLOCKHOUSE (LANGEMARK 1.10,000)	HhJ

2353 Wt. W2544/1454 700,000 5/15 D. D. & L. A.D.S.S./Forms/C. 2118.

WAR DIARY (Sheet 2)
or
~~INTELLIGENCE~~ SUMMARY.

(Erase heading not required.)

Army Form C. 2118.

Instructions regarding War Diaries and Intelligence Summaries are contained in F. S. Regs., Part II. and the Staff Manual respectively. Title pages will be prepared in manuscript.

Place	Date	Hour	Summary of Events and Information	Remarks and references to Appendices
	18th-19th (Contd)		Total casualties for tour. Officers - T/Lieut Col. Morris killed, 2/Lt Ford wounded Other ranks - 15 killed 66 wounded	HLJ
	19th 20th		Battalion is relieved by 4th Worcesters and embusses at BOESINGHE for DUBLIN CAMP (Ref A.10.d. Sheet 28 N.W.)	HLJ
	23rd		One 2/Lieut reinforcement joins Battalion	HLJ
	24th		Battalion moves into Brigade Support at DULWICH CAMP (B 9 c. Sheet 28 N.W.)	HLJ
	27th		" entrains at ELVERDINGHE Station for PROVEN AREA NO. 3 and marches to PORCHESTER CAMP (E.6.b.6.6. Sheet 27) Divisional Area 10% rejoin Battalion at Station	HLJ
	28th		Majority of 10% Corps Area and draft join Battalion - 11 2/Lieuts and 114 Other ranks	HLJ
			Honours & Awards Bar to M.C. - Capt J. A. W. Wilson MILITARY CROSS - 2/Lt J. R. Mumford MILITARY MEDALS - Sig: Sgt Wintour; Sgt Fox "D" Coy; " Kelly "A" "; " Weeks "B" "; L/Cpl Fitzgerald "B" Coy; " Bates "D" "; Pte Boyce "D" "; " Mason "D" "; " Green "A" "; " Hanbury "B" "	HLJ

Confidential

War Diary

of

16th Middlesex Regt

From 1.9.17 to 30.9.17

Volume XXIII

Instructions regarding War Diaries and Intelligence Summaries are contained in F. S. Regs., Part II. and the Staff Manual respectively. Title pages will be prepared in manuscript.

WAR DIARY
or
~~INTELLIGENCE SUMMARY.~~
(Erase heading not required.)

16th MIDDLESEX RGT
29TH DIVISION
XIV CORPS

Army Form C. 2118.

Volume XXIII Page 28

Place	Date	Hour	Summary of Events and Information	Remarks and references to Appendices
	September 1917			
	1st		Battalion is in Camp at E. 5. b. 6 6 (Sheet 27).	[illegible]
	7th		Battalion, less details proceed at 6·50am to PROVEN STATION to entrain for ELVERDINGHE, CAMBRIDGE CAMP B.9 a. 88 for work under C.R.E. XIV Corps. Road-making in forward area (Ref. Congratulated on good work done and amount of material salved	[illegible]
	8th		Reinforcements received week ending 7th. - 7 Second Lieuts 106 other ranks	[illegible]
	10th		Battalion less details entrains at ELVERDINGHE at 8am having finished work under C.R.E XIV Corps and returns to Camp at E. 5. b. 6. 6	[illegible]
	16th		Battalion marches to HERZEELE for Brigade training D. 9 a. 8 4 (Sheet 27 NE). 1 officer + 64 other ranks remaining in PORCHESTER CAMP E. 5 b 6 6	[illegible]
	18th		Capt J.A.W. WILSON. M.C. and PTE. A. BOYCE decorated by GEN CAPELLE (Commanding 1st FRENCH ARMY) with the CROIX DU GUERRE for gallantry during operations AUGUST 10th - 13th	[illegible]
	19th		Battalion completes Brigade training and marches back to PORCHESTER CAMP.	[illegible]
	20th		Battalion, less 10% Corps Depot proceeds by train from PROVEN at 14·40 to ELVERDINGHE and is billeted in Tents, Bivouacs and Dug-outs in CHARTERHOUSE CAMP (EMILE FARM) B 9 c 8 5 (Sheet 28 NW) Strength 22 officers 668 other ranks	[illegible]
	21st		About 16 40 a squadron of hostile aeroplanes flew over Camp dropping about 20 bombs 1 other rank wounded, no material damage done. Reinforcements received week ending 21st 1 Lieut. 31 other ranks.	[illegible]
	23rd		Battalion employed on TRACK 11 (much material salved	[illegible]

Sheet II

WAR DIARY
or
INTELLIGENCE SUMMARY.
(Erase heading not required.)

Army Form C. 2118.

Instructions regarding War Diaries and Intelligence Summaries are contained in F. S. Regs., Part II. and the Staff Manual respectively. Title pages will be prepared in manuscript.

Place	Date	Hour	Summary of Events and Information	Remarks and references to Appendices
	September 1917			
	24th		Battalion employed on TRACK II (much material salved)	
			15 O.R. despatched for temporary attachment to work under LONDON FIELD COY R.E building encampment huts	
			Carrying party 1 officer 40 O.R working under LONDON FIELD COY R.E clearing Railhead RUGBY DUMP C 1 a.3.1	
	25th		Working party 1 officer 40 O.R (RUGBY DUMP) Casualty - 1 O.R slightly gassed	
	27th		About 8.30pm enemy put one H.E into Camp wounding 5 O.R	
	28th		Working party 1 officer 40 O.R (RUGBY DUMP)	
	29th/30th		Battalion less "C" & "D" Coys moves off from CHARTERHOUSE CAMP (B.9 c 8.5) and relieves the 1st ROYAL DUBLIN FUSILIERS in the front line (right sub-sector of Divisional front) LANGEMARK. Route - TRACK II HUNTER ST HUNTER SWITCH Battalion H^D Q^rs at U. 23 c 1 1	
			"C" & "D" Coys move to DULWICH CAMP at B. 8 c 6.9	

8353 Wt. W2544/1454 700,000 5/15 D. D. & L. A.D.S.S./Forms/C. 2118.

86/39

Confidential

War Diary

of

16th Middlesex Regt

From 1.10.17 to 31.10.17

Volume XXIV

Vol 24

Instructions regarding War Diaries and Intelligence Summaries are contained in F. S. Regs., Part II. and the Staff Manual respectively. Title pages will be prepared in manuscript.

WAR DIARY
or
~~INTELLIGENCE SUMMARY.~~
(*Erase heading not required.*)

16th Middlesex Regt. Army Form C. 2118.
29th Division
VI Corps
Volume XXIV Page 29.

Place	Date	Hour	Summary of Events and Information	Remarks and references to Appendices
	October 1917.			
	1st		"A" + "B" Coys in front line (right sub-sector of Divisional front) LANGEMARK. Battalion HdQrs CROSS ROADS LANGEMARK. U. 23. c. 01.15.	
			"C" + "D" Coys in DULWICH CAMP. B. 8. c. 6.9.	
			"C" + "D" Coys relieve "A" + "B" in front line, latter Coys returning to DULWICH CAMP. B. 8. c. 6.9.	
			Casualties:- Other ranks Killed 7. wounded 17.	
	3rd		Casualties:- " " 1 " 6 missing 1.	
	3rd/4th		"C" + "D" Coys relieved by 1st ROYAL DUBLIN FUSILIERS in front line.	
			2 platoons "B" Coy (Strength LT. B. FOSTER. 2/LT. R.W.P. MITCHELL 80 other ranks) attached to 1st RDFs as liasson party on right flank with 4th Division and moved up to front line with them for offensive operation on 4th	
			Casualties:- LT. FOSTER and 2/LT. MITCHELL wounded. Other ranks, killed 9. wounded 25. missing 6.	
			Honours:- L/Cpl. J. H. HANBURY - D.C.M. PTE. W. MUNDAY - MILITARY MEDAL.	
	6th/7th		Balance rejoin Battalion.	
	6th		Carrying Parties AU BON GITE (U. 28. b. 2. 0.) BROMBEKE. Strength 2 Officers 88 other ranks.	
			Digging Party. Commandant ELVERDINGHE. Strength 100.	
			GOUVY FARM. " 30.	
	7th		Battalion moves from DULWICH CAMP to HARROW CAMP. ELVERDINGHE.	
	7th to 17th		Divisional 10% 1 officer (2/LT. GREEN) and 30 other ranks attached to D.A.C. for man handling guns into position in forward area.	
			Casualties:- Other ranks 2 killed 6 wounded.	

Instructions regarding War Diaries and Intelligence Summaries are contained in F. S. Regs., Part II. and the Staff Manual respectively. Title pages will be prepared in manuscript.

WAR DIARY
or
~~INTELLIGENCE SUMMARY.~~
(*Erase heading not required.*)

Sheet II

Army Form C. 2118.

Place	Date	Hour	Summary of Events and Information	Remarks and references to Appendices
	October 1917			
	9th		Battalion is told off as Counter-attack battalion in operations of 86th Infantry Brigade. Battalion less two platoons "B" Coy move off at 2am and dig in on PILKEM RIDGE around the guns. Battalion Hd Qrs at CORK HOUSE C.3.a 1.3. Zero hour 5-20 am. Battalion is ordered to move forward at 8am. Battalion moves forward in Artillery formation "C" "D" "A" "B" through LANGEMARK and digs in in front of BLOCKHOUSE at U.18.c 4.5. No casualties during advance. In afternoon Battalion is called upon to reinforce front line which was being counter-attacked. Battalion starts to move up but is stopped as the reason for reinforcing has ceased to exist. Battalion digs in again in front of CONDÉ HOUSES U.13.a 2 9. Battalion is ordered to take over right half of Brigade front in evening, and does so. Battalion Hd Qrs OLGA HOUSE U.18.b 60.15. No counter attack is made on Battalion while in the line. Brigade on left counter-attacked by enemy across BROMBEEK but attack did not reach Battalion front. Casualties:- 2/LT EDDY killed, other ranks 5 killed 62 wounded, 2 missing. Honours:- 2/LT (A/CAPT) S.R.F. HIDE (attached 86th T.M.B) MILITARY CROSS. L/C E. WHITMARSH. PTE F. STUBBS. MILITARY MEDALS.	[illegible]
	10th/11th		Battalion is relieved in front line by 10TH SHERWOOD FORESTERS and returns for short time to support lines behind and in front of OLGA HOUSE U.18.b.60.15, (Battalion Hd Qrs at U.18.c.4.5) and is relieved by 7TH BORDER REGT. Relief complete by 12 midnight and Battalion is billeted for few hours in Camp at ELVERDINGHE CHATEAU	[illegible]
	11th	11am	Battalion entrains at ELVERDINGHE for PROVEN AREA + is billeted in PERA CAMP E.16.a.8.5. (SHEET 27).	[illegible]
	16th		Battalion leaves XIV Corps and 5th Army + is transferred with Division to VI Corps 3rd Army + proceeds by train from POPERINGHE (HOUPOUTRE SIDING) at 5-30pm. Congratulatory + farewell messages received from Army and Corps Commanders.	[illegible]
	17th to 31st		Battalion detrains at BEAUMETZ 7-30am + marches to No. 5. CAMP HENDECOURT X.16.d.4.8 (SHEET 51.c) is billeted in huts + carries on training.	[illegible]

2353 Wt. W2544/1454 700,000 5/15 D. D. & L. A.D.S.S./Forms/C. 2118.

Instructions regarding War Diaries and Intelligence Summaries are contained in F. S. Regs., Part II. and the Staff Manual respectively. Title pages will be prepared in manuscript.

WAR DIARY
or
INTELLIGENCE SUMMARY.
(Erase heading not required.)

16th Middlesex Regt
29th Division
VI Corps.
Volume ~~XXV~~ Page 30
Vol 25

Army Form C. 2118.

56/9

Place	Date	Hour	Summary of Events and Information	Remarks and references to Appendices
November 1917				
	1st/16th		Battalion in No 5 Camp HENDICOURT X16 d.4.8 (Sheet 57c)	
	17th/18th		Battalion leaves HENDICOURT & marches to and entrains at BOISLIEUX-AU-MONT at 12.25 am.	
	18th		" detrains at PERONNE. Marches to Hut Camp at HAUT ALLAINES.	
	18th	7.25 pm	Battn marches to EQUANCOURT via MOISLAINS - NURLU & FINS.	
	19th	0100	Battn arrives EQUANCOURT - Battle stores issued.	
	20th	0215	" moves off from EQUANCOURT via FINS to place of Assembly Q23 ~~d~~ & forms up in diamond formation	
	20th	0620	Zero hour!!	
	"	0630	Battn moves forward in diamond formation to R7 central and lies up in trenches waiting for capture of 1st & 2nd lines of HINDENBURG & HINDENBURG Support.	
		1040	Battn is ordered to advance & moves off in diamond formation - Battn being advanced guard to Brigade: C Coy forming the vanguard - A Coy left flank guard - B Coy the Right flank guard and D Coy the main guard. Bn HQ + 1 Sect T.M.B., 2 Sections M.G. Coy at head of main guard.	
			A certain number of gaps found in the wire and great delay - caused crossing the Hindenburg Trenches.	
		1130	Hindenburg Support is passed and Battn slows up in the valley to allow 1st R.G.L.I. on left and 2nd R.Fs on right to close up.	
			Advance on NINE WOOD is then proceeded with. Until then there had been no opposition and only desultory shell fire. No casualties had been incurred.	
			When about half way up the slope of PREMY CHAPELLE HILL Battn comes under rifle fire. The advance is pushed on and Germans are seen reinforcing the line from MARCOING. Firing and advancing by Platoons and afterwards by sectional rushes the attack is pressed home with as little checking as possible.	
			A Coy leaving for S.W. side of NINE WOOD, lead by Capt J.A.W. WILSON M.C. made ground rapidly.	
			C Coy under Capt D.B. TUCK having broken back enemy outpost line, reorganised in a Quarry and attacked the South side of NINE WOOD.	
			D Coy under 2nd Lt A.L BOBBY by then had come up into line and together with B Coy, skirted S.E corner of wood and attacked ^two lines^ trenches at L10d.74 & 11275. on E side of wood.	
			On the way the 2nd R.Fs were held up by M.G at L17a.8.3. Major E.R. Hill, commanding B Coy, dropped 1 platoon under Lt H.M. Trower to protect his right flank. Lt TROWER immediately attacked the gun on the flank and captured it, removing the cause of check which allowed the 2nd R.Fs to continue the advance.	
			The 2 lines of trenches which were the objectives of B & D Coys were captured without much difficulty - the 2 RFs coming up on the Right flank.	
			At the same time A Coy made a push through the centre side of the wood and appeared at the East side of it and occupied a portion of the Sunken Road L10d.6.7. to L11c.3.8.	

2353 Wt. W2544/1454 700,000 5/15 D. D. & L. A.D.S.S./Forms/C. 2118.

Instructions regarding War Diaries and Intelligence Summaries are contained in F. S. Regs., Part II. and the Staff Manual respectively. Title pages will be prepared in manuscript.

WAR DIARY
or
INTELLIGENCE SUMMARY.

(Erase heading not required.)

Army Form C. 2118.

Place	Date	Hour	Summary of Events and Information	Remarks and references to Appendices
	20th	1330	The objective of the Battn was won. The Battn was on its objective by 13.00 and reported as completely captured at 1330 The 1st R.G.L.I. then came up on the left flank and connected up round EAST & N.E side of wood. During the attack there was no close support from Artillery fire but great assistance was rendered by the TANK Corps. 4 Tanks, under Capt Ingham, were detailed to the Brigade and moved with us during the advance. Skirting NINE wood they proceeded to shell the village of NOYELLES. 4 other Tanks, under Capt R.G. Davies, 24th Coy, joined in the fight after they had finished the capture of the Hindenburg Support line. They rendered great assistance and did not withdraw until the capture of the wood was complete. Consolidation A Coy in the Sunken road to the East of the wood B & D Coys the German Trench, which was merely a dummy trench in Rear L.10.d.7.4 to L.11.c.7.5 C Coy remained in support in wood in quarry at L.10.d.4.7. Battn HQ moved to house in centre of wood. L.10.d.1.3. As soon as objectives had been captured patrols were pushed out to NOYELLES. 1 platoon under 2nd Lt Morris, with the assistance of a Tank made for the cross roads North of NOYELLES. He advanced through the village and reported it clear of enemy. Another platoon under 2nd Lt Whittington went to the crossing at L.6.C.2.3 – reporting bridge blown up but light railway bridge still in tact. The 2nd R.F's came up later & the bridgehead was handed over to them – the platoon returning to the battalion 1 platoon under 2nd Lt Green went out to cross roads at L.5.c.2.3 and consolidated the post. The post was relieved after dark by 1 platoon under 2nd Lt Philpotts A squadron of cavalry were reported to be in position in the village of NOYELLES but their exact whereabouts was not located so the post was reinforced by a 2nd platoon of C Coy under 2nd Lt Kirkham who occupied edge of village at L.5.c.6.4 facing North. Contrary reports and rumours kept coming in as to position on right of NOYELLES – i.e. L.6.c.2.3 so a post of regimental snipers was placed at the light Railway bridge. They sniped from the hedge L.6.C.2.5 until driven in by enemy counter attack at dawn next morning.	
		1500	About this time the Cavalry came up to NINE WOOD and went through in direction of CANTAING about 4 p.m. – Coming back again behind NINE Wood before dark. Night passed very quietly.	
	21.	0700	Enemy attacked NOYELLES – a party of about 500 – attacking the post at L.5.C.2.3. and drove the 2 platoons in. These 2 platoons retired up the road to NINE Wood and finding a gap with the 1/Guernsey Light Infantry's line at L.10.b.4.3. filled the gap and consolidated. A party of the enemy were causing trouble from a ditch at L.10.b.8.8. so 2/Lt KIRKHAM went out alone with a Lewis Gun & drove them off. Consolidation was completed without further trouble.	
		1250	Orders were received from Bde to take over line of left Coy of Royal Fusiliers. At 1300 B Coy took over new line down to Sunken Road at L.11.d.5.5 and D Coy extended their front to include B Coy's old position. Meanwhile enemy occupied NOYELLES and developed an attack against NINE WOOD. This was stopped by frontal fire of A Coy when within 300x of the wood & by enfilade fire from B Coy. The enemy did not push the attack and finally retired to NOYELLES.	

A353 Wt. W2544/1454 700,000 5/15 D. D. & L. A.D.S.S./Forms/C. 2118.

3

WAR DIARY
or
INTELLIGENCE SUMMARY.
(Erase heading not required.)

Instructions regarding War Diaries and Intelligence Summaries are contained in F. S. Regs., Part II. and the Staff Manual respectively. Title pages will be prepared in manuscript.

Army Form C. 2118.

Place	Date	Hour	Summary of Events and Information	Remarks and references to Appendices
	21		About 1:30 pm orders from Brigade were received that Bn was being relieved by 2nd Yorks & Lancs: & to hand over post at L.5.c.2.3 correct. A [patrol of one] platoon under 2/Lt Phil Potts was sent to the cross roads but as enemy was there in force were unable to attain their object but had a fairly hot engagement with the enemy, causing several casualties to them. When the platoon returned with this report Scouts were sent out to locate enemy's new position. These men returned with the report that the cross roads were then unoccupied by the enemy. Capt Tuck, O.C. 'C' Coy then went to cross roads and occupied the position with 2 platoons and post was handed over intact to 2nd Yorks & Lancs. Relief was complete at 9 pm and battn marched to billets in MARCOING. L22.a.9.3.	
	22		Bn received orders to relieve a Bn of 88th Bde in right sector of Division. At 4.40 pm Bn marched to MASNIERES & relieved 1st Newfoundland Regt in Support & came under orders of 88th Bde. B & D Coys in reserve line astride CAMBRAI & RUMILLY Roads. A & C Coys in cellars in MASNIERES – being the Counterattack Coys. Bn HQ in Catacombs. During night Bn employed in digging reserve defences & communications to front line. 1/Lancs Fus: taking over left sector of 88th Bde front from 1st Essex Regt.	
	23		Battn. is relieved by 2nd Royal Fus: in Support and	
	23	4 pm	took over central section of Brigade front N.E of MASNIERES from 2nd Hants, A.B. & D coys in front line, C coy in support HQ in cellars 27 a 0.9. Arrangements made to attempt peaceful penetration at 1.30 am our immediate objective being the house at 21 a 5.1 and the trench E. of it. The 1st Lanc Fusil on the left attempted to penetrate up the CAMBRAI ROAD at 11.30 pm & as their effort resulted in complete failure, orders arrived 12.15 am from Brigade cancelling our attempt.	
	24th		Consolidating trench system from RUMILLY RD 21.c 4.9 to 27 a 9.8.	
	25th		Attack planned on the enemy positions in front of RUMILLY. 87th Bde on left of CAMBRAI Rd. 86th Bde on right, 1st Lanc Fusil on left of Brigade section, M.x on right. Objectives road from 21 a 8.5 to windmill 21 b 3.1 & a defensive flank on the right thrown back to our present front line about 21 c 9.3. Attack postponed till tomorrow.	
	26th		Attack cancelled. 9.0 pm relieved by 1st Lanc Fusil. Bn goes into Bde reserve A & C coys astride the CAMBRAI & RUMILLY RDS. in reserve line. B & D coys counter attack. Coys in cellars in MASNIERES.	
	27th		Brigade reorganises sectors for defense. 2 Battn in front line. 2 in reserve. 9 pm Bn takes over right sector of front line from the 1st R.G.L.I & 1 coy of 1st L.F. from the canal at 28 c 2.0 to 21 c 6.3 being in touch with the left of 20th Div on the Canal Bank. Main line of defence running N. from 27 d 2.0 to solitary house at 27 b 2.3 swinging back from here to 21 c 6.3 with outposts at MON PLAISIR FARM & the bridge at 28 c 2.0. HQ established at the house on canal bank 27 c 4.8.	
	28th/29th		Consolidating trenches, firing lines made very nearly continuous & 2 communication trenches out. Disposition. B coy the canal to 27 d 2.9 having at night 1 Platoon at MON PLAISIR FM & 1 L.G. & 1 bombing post at the bridge head at 28 c 2.0. by day outpost consists of 1 L.G. post at MON PLAISIR FM with a support post at 27 d 8.8, remainder retired into Coy support. C coy 27 d 2.9 to 27 a 9.9 all in front line owing to support trench not having yet been dug. D coy 27 a 9.9 to 21 c 6.3 one Platoon in support 21 c 0.0. A coy Battn Reserve. 2 Platoons 27 a 6.4 to 27 a 8.8, 1 platoon 27 c 7.7.	

#353 Wt. W2544/1454 700,000 5/15 D. D. & L. A.D.S.S./Forms/C. 2118.

Army Form C. 2118.

WAR DIARY
or
INTELLIGENCE SUMMARY.

(*Erase heading not required.*)

Instructions regarding War Diaries and Intelligence Summaries are contained in F. S. Regs., Part II. and the Staff Manual respectively. Title pages will be prepared in manuscript.

Place	Date	Hour	Summary of Events and Information	Remarks and references to Appendices
	30th		The enemy having been shelling the back areas for sometime put down his barrage at 7 am on MASNIERES	
		7.35am	enemy M.G. barrage commenced	
		7.40a	lull in all firing	
		7.45a	bombardment of our front line trenches.	
		7.55am	enemy guns lifted & MASNIERES was again barraged.	
		8.15am	enemy infantry attack developed. thin lines of skirmishers came down the hill between CREVECOEUR & RUMILLY followed by thicker waves behind, the same formation was adopted S of the canal against the 20th Division. Our rifle fire & L.G fire slowed up the attack & finally stopped it at a range of about 400 to 500 yds. S of the Canal the enemy hardly checked at all.	
		8.25	The S.O.S was put up in various parts of our line when the enemy was about 600 yds distant, but there was no response by the artillery. Advance Post MON PLAISIR Fm driven in having driven in the front line of 20th Div. the enemy came on in masses S of the Canal	
		8.45	Reserve Platoon of A coy sent from 27c 7.7 to the right of B coy to hold the Canal Bank at the bend about 27 d 0.0	
		9.0	The 20th Div apparently driven back altogether the 2 remaining reserve Platoons of A coy advanced up one to hold the lock bridge 27c 5.5 & the other the small foot bridge 27.c 2.9. meanwhile these bridges were each held by about 5 men of the H.Q party. The Regtl snipers occupying the houses S of the lock 27c 45.45	
			A good defensive flank was thus formed facing S. the support platoon of D coy was also brought back into Regtl reserve at 27 a 6.4. The enemy came on in masses S of the canal going W. leaving LES RUES VERTES on their right.	
			About 10.0am OC Z coy R.F reported to me with 2 coys R.F reinforcements at the small foot bridge 27c 2.9. I ordered him to occupy at once the cross roads at 32 b. 0.7 with 1 Coy & the S edge of LES RUES VERTES with the other. He was very slow getting across the bridge, finally the 2nd i/c R.F came up & I explained the situation to him. The 2 coys took about half an hour to cross the bridge & lay down in the marsh the other side for about another half hour. They then advanced on the cross roads 32 b 0 7 but by that time the enemy had got there & the 2 coys were driven back. They retired across the Canal back into MASNIERES. Meanwhile seeing that LES RUES VERTES was likely to be captured I sent the Adjutant Capt JAMES with a few men to the Brigade Dump in LES RUES VERTES to shift as much ammunition as possible from the Dump to the N side of the Canal, the Dump was shortly in the hands of the enemy but the Staff Capt with the Adjt & a few men drove the	

Instructions regarding War Diaries and Intelligence Summaries are contained in F. S. Regs., Part II. and the Staff Manual respectively. Title pages will be prepared in manuscript.

WAR DIARY
or
INTELLIGENCE SUMMARY.
(*Erase heading not required.*)

Army Form C. 2118.

Place	Date	Hour	Summary of Events and Information	Remarks and references to Appendices
	30		enemy back & some of the ammunition was brought across. Also in view of expected shelling I cleared all the ammunition out of Battn HQ to prevent it getting buried when the house was knocked down.	
		11 am	Capt FEATHERSTONE was wounded & several men of A coy made casualties in establishing the bridge head post at the LOCK. Lieut DEEVES had already posted Regtl snipers in the houses S of the Canal at 27c 45·46 who had excellent practice. Lt LITTLE from 10% placed i/c A coy 12.30 pm. Bn HQ was evacuated in view of the fact that enemy artillery were coming into action about 32 b. The men occupying Reserve trench just to N.W. of the house.	
		12.35	Battn HQ shelled by heavy trench mortars & the front of the house blown in	
		2.45	1 Platoon RF (1 officer 15 men) found at Lock Bridge having been sent up by Bde as reinforcements. I placed in close support under OC A coy in trench 27c 6·6.	
		3.0 pm	Owing to continual M.G fire & sniping at [illegible], HQ moved to Reserve trench E of Sugar Factory 27a 5·2. During the day B, C & D Coys in original front line were being badly enfiladed by field guns at close range & occasionally attacked by thin waves of infantry, all day hostile aircraft were flying low over our trenches, continually fired at but none brought down. None of our aircraft seen and artillery support.	
		6 pm	Battn HQ returned to old HQ on the Canal Bank for the night returning to same trench 27a 5·2 before dawn. The T.M gun at 27c 9·7 had been hit by shrapnel early in the day & put out of action. During the night supplies of water and ammunition got up to front line. Quiet night.	

Casualties.

	Officers	Other ranks
Killed	1	28
wounded	10 (1 at Duty)	110
missing	–	38

1 officer & 21 other ranks attd Kent R.E's MISSING

Capt B. Knowles R.A.M.C attd wounded (at Duty)

2nd Lt A L Bobby Killed
" A.G. Chittington wounded
" A.K. Mellenfield "
" J.B. Newman "
" G.H. Larkins " (died of wounds)
" S.L. Davies accidentally wounded
Lt Col J. Ambes-Robertson D.S.O. M.C wounded (at Duty)
Capt E. Featherstone wounded
2nd Lt J.H. Deeves "
" A. Gossen "
" G.H. Wykstead "
" J.W. Lane missing (attd Kent R.E's)

2353 Wt. W2544/1454 700,000 5/15 D. D. & L. A.D.S.S./Forms/C. 2118.

- - - - - Platoon position morning of 30th Nov.
- - - - - " " evening of 1st Dec.
O Battn HQ position morning of 30th Nov
O " " " evening of 1st Dec.

- - - Platoon 20th & 21st Nov.
O HQ 20th & 21st Nov.

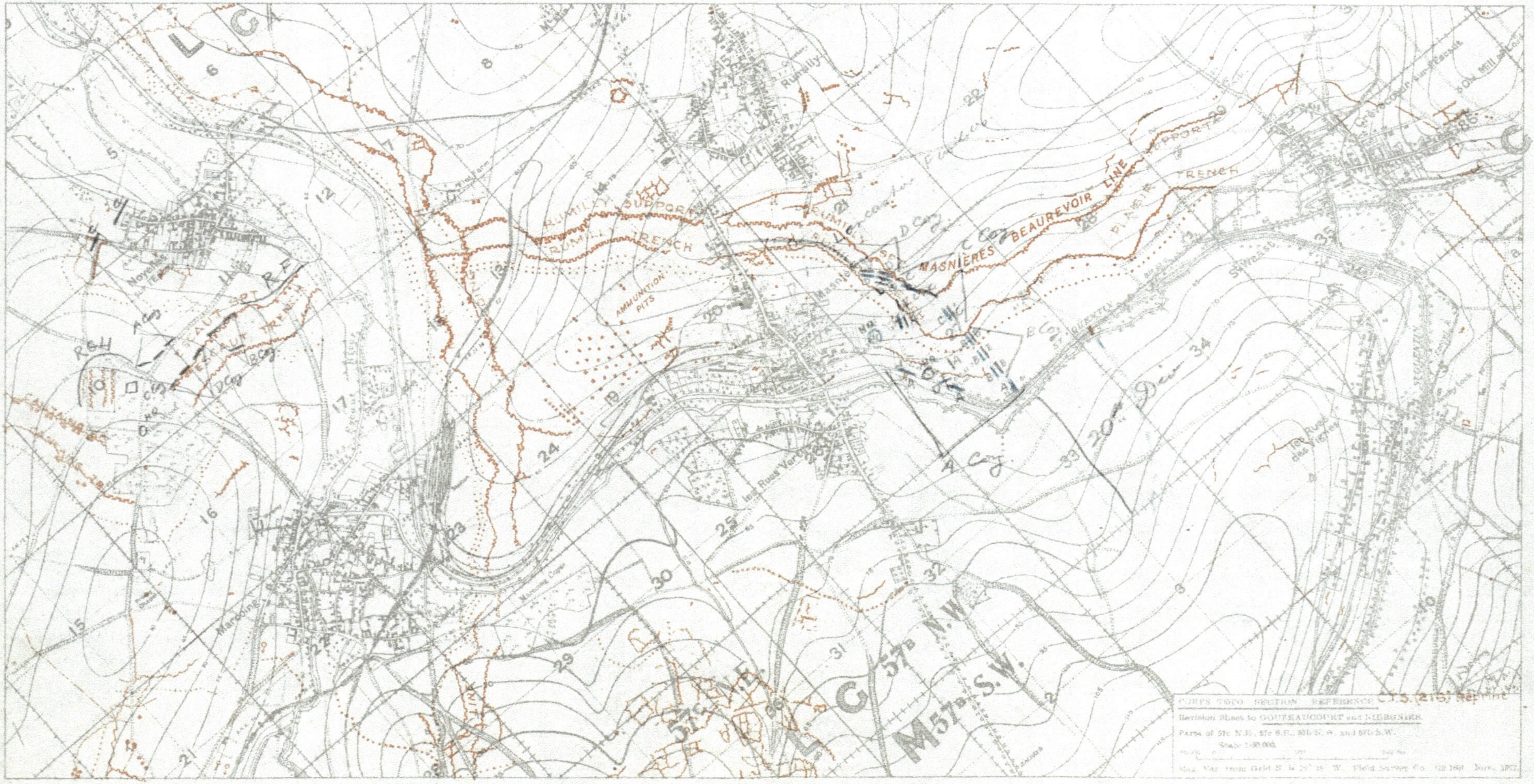

MESSAGE FORM.

To No.

1. I am at.................................. (Note:—Either give Map Reference or mark your position by a 'X' on the Map on back.)

2. My Line runs...

3. My Platoon / Company is at..and is consolidating.

4. My Platoon / Company is at..and has consolidated.

5. Am held up by (a) M.G. / (b) Wire at....................(Place where you are).

6. Enemy holding strong point...............................

7. I am in touch with....................................on Right / Left at............

8. I am not in touch with....................................on Right. / Left.

9. Am shelled from.......................................

10. Am in need of :—

11. Counter Attack forming at.....................................

12. Hostile (a) Battery / (b) Machine Gun / (c) Trench Mortar active at.......................................

13. Reinforcements wanted at...

14. I estimate my present strength at................rifles

15. Have captured.......................

16. Prisoners belong to..

17. Add any other useful information here :—

Name....................................

Platoon....................................

Time..........................m. Company....................................

Date.......................1917. Battalion....................................

(A). Carry no maps or papers which may be of value to the Enemy.

(B). Give no information if captured, except the following, which you are bound to give :—

Name and Rank.

(C). Collect all captured maps and papers and send them in at once.

OPERATION ORDERS
BY
LIEUT.COL.J.FORBES-ROBERTSON.D.S.O.,M.C.
COMMANDING 16TH.BATTALION MIDDLESEX REGIMENT.

NOVEMBER.19TH.1917.

On the ~~said~~ "Z" day the 3rd.Corps will attack with the assistance of Tanks conjunction with other troops.
The 6th,12th,and 20th.Divisions will capture BLUE and BROWN LINES, after which the 29th.Division will pass through the above Divisions and capture the RED LINE.
The 86th.Brigade on the left will capture NINE WOOD and trenches east of it to the ST.QUENTIN CANAL,boundaries as shewn on the map.
The 6th.Division will form a left defensive flank up to PREMY-CHAPPELLE HILL.

The advance to the front line trenches. 1

The 86th.Brigade will assemble in Q.25. at an hour to be notified later.
The Middlesex Regiment assembling in Q.23.d.& 24.c.
At zero the Brigade will advance to our front line trench. The Middlesex Regiment in PLOUGH TRENCH & PLOUGH SUPPORT from R.7.a.4.5. to R.7.b.6.3. & Q.12.b.8.1. to R.7.d.25.30.
Battalion Head Quarters at R.7.b.2.3.
R.G.L.I. on thr left and the 2/Royal Fusiliers on the right.
On arrival in PLOUGH TRENCH "C" Company will push on to German front line trench called- RIDGE TRENCH about R.2.a.and the scouts under Lt. Deeves will push on to BROWN LINE about L.27.d.
"B" Company will be accomodated in PLOUGH TRENCH from R.7.b.2.6. to R.7.b.6.3.
"A" Company from R.7.b.1.6. to R.7.a.5.4.
"D" Company in PLOUGH SUPPORT from R.7.c.9.9. to R.7.c.5.8.
One section M.G.Coy, one section T.M.B,and one section R.E. will be accomodated in R.7.d.2.8.
The Battalion will remain in this position until ordered to advance.

The advance to the attack. 2

The advance will be sounded on Bugle ~~____~~ and a runner of each Company having previously reported to Hd.Qrs.will retutn with a message.
The Battalion will advance in diamond formation.
"C" Coy.will form Vanguard,"B"Coy plus 2 Machine Guns will form the right flank guard.
"A" Coy will form the left flank guard,"D"Coy plus 2 Machine Guns, plus 1 section T.M.B,plus 1 section R.Es.will form the Mainguard.
Battn.H.Qrs.at the head of the Mainguard.
The bearing of the advance will be 45 degrees magnetic.
The right flank guard keeping to the left of COUILLET WOOD.

OBJECTIVES.

"C" Coy South edge of NINE WOOD leaving Lewis Gun posts at South edge end of the two Rides running N.W.through the wood - push on round to E.side of wood up to the sunken Road and attack the two trenches in L.11.c. from the W.end.
"A" Coy The Quarry outside the wood at L.16.a.- push on down the Ride through wood running N.E.and occupy the E.side of the wood between the Road junction L.10.d.3.8. to where the trench meets wood at L.10.d.7.4.
"B" Coy The Quarry in L.16.c.The trench in L.16.b.The Strong Point in L.17.a.and will assist the covering fire the Royal Fusiliers attacking the N.side of MARCOING VILLAGE.
As the R.Fusiliers come up to "B" Coy at the above points these will be evacuated by us,and "B" Coy will then occupy the Southern of the two German trenches in L.11.b.7.2. to L.10.d.7.1.
"D" Coy will wheel round S.E.corner of NINE WOOD and attack two German trenches from the wood on the left to L.11.c.7.5. where the wire crosses the trench.
"A" Coy providing the mopping up party for the southern of these two trenches .
"D" Coys final position will be in the Northern trench from L.11.c.7.5. to L.10.d.7.4.

REORGANISATION.

If possible the Battalion will be reorganised as follows:-
"D" Coy in the Northern trench between the points given above.
"B" Coy in the Southern-trench " " " "

"A" Coy on the E. ~~side~~ edge of the wood between the points given above, with an outpost in the Sunken Road at L.11.c.?.8.
"C" Coy in the S.E. portion of wood.
Battn.Hd.Qrs.in S.E. corner of wood.

AID POST.
In the Quarry on the S.W.Side of wood to which place also all prisoners will be sent.

Brigade Hd.Qrs. During the attack will halt at L.27.a.2.., and on the objectives being gained will move to the cross Roads at L.22.a.8.8. At this point there will be a Brigade runner post until the Bde.Hd.Qrs. arrive.

The Royal Fusiliers will occupy from our right to the ST.QUENTIN CANAL.
The R.G.L.I.will occupy from our left to the Northern part of the wood.
~~The Lancs.Fusiliers will be the counter attack Battalion and will be in reserve at L.10.c. to L.16.d.central.~~
The dividing line being the Ride running S.W.& N.E.through the middle of the wood. This position will be consolidated facing the NOYELLES.
After the position has been occupied a patrol of one platoon will be sent by "D" Coy to the Cross Roads at L.5.c.2.3. The Lanc. Fusiliers will be the counter attack Bn & will be in reserve at L.16.c to L.16.d. central.

TANKS.
Sixteen Tanks will assist in the attack on NINE WOOD , 2 tanks will go along the southern side of the wood, one tank through the centre, one tank round the N.side of the wood and the other 12 will join in the attack as required.

3 (Cavalry pass through) When the 20th.Division has won all the objectives the cavalry will go through.
The first cavalry Division will go through the 86th.Bde.moving on NOYELLES and N. of it.
Every endeavour must be made to leave the Roads clear for the cavalry.

4 (Relieved by 6th Div.) If the cavalry operations are successful the 86th.Bde.will be relieved by a Brigade of the 6th.Division and will move into Divisional reserve in MARCOING and the trenches E. of it.
At dawn next day i.e. Z plus 1 day the 86th.Brigade will take over and consolidate a defensive position at H.19.a. to LA BELLE ETOILE B.25.c.

5 (The advance to occupy final position) The 87th.Brigade being on the left and the 20th.Division on the right.

1st.Phase. The advance to the front line trenches.

2nd. " The advance to the attack.

3rd. " Cavalry go through.

4th. " Relieved by the 6th.Division.

5th. " The advance to occupy final position at H.19.a.

(Signed) H.M.James.
Capt & Adjt.

Confidential

War Diary

of

16th Middlesex Regt.

From 1.12.17 to 31.12.17.

Volume XXVI.

Vol 26

Army Form C. 2118.

WAR DIARY
or
INTELLIGENCE SUMMARY.
(Erase heading not required.)

Instructions regarding War Diaries and Intelligence Summaries are contained in F. S. Regs., Part II. and the Staff Manual respectively. Title pages will be prepared in manuscript.

16th Middlesex Rgt
29th Division
Volume XXVI Page 31

Place	Date	Hour	Summary of Events and Information	Remarks and references to Appendices
	December 1st 1917			
		7.30am	Heavy attack on LES RUES VERTES from S.E. Preceded by bombardment of our line. Did much good work enfilading the enemy's attacking troops. Enemy aircraft again very active none of ours visible. Bn HQ shelled by field guns.	[illegible]
		11 am	Trench enfiladed by battery at 32 b 0 3, 14 casualties. HQ retire to Sugar Factory. B coy heavily shelled by heavy T.M. behind MON PLAISIR FM. A new Stokes Gun brought up in the night was outranged. Enemy advanced to the attack at intervals but were always completely checked & nowhere got closer than 200 yds & were not in any numbers.	[illegible]
		3 pm	Enemy drove in our outposts in the houses across the Lock Bridge.	[illegible]
		5.30pm	Enemy occupied the Canal bank at the Lock Bridge in some strength. Officer i/c sent message for reinforcements which were not required. Until situation was cleared up Reserve Platoon D coy brought to Lock Bridge & Platoon of C coy taken out of firing line & put into Bn Reserve at 27 a 6.4. The reinforcements that actually did arrive consisted of 1 Cpl & 2 men of the S.W.B with a Lewis Gun. About 10 am and again at 3 pm our artillery shelled the German Guns S. of the canal, on both occasions the enemy gun teams were brought up at the trot & there was every indication of the enemy artillery retiring. Our fire died down & the enemy gun teams were taken away, the guns remaining in action. The enemy infantry generally were very nervous, their advances were not carried out with determination & showed no inclination to face our infantry fire.	[illegible]
		7.30pm	Orders received from Bde to evacuate between 11.40 am & 12.15 pm, via the Chateau MASNIERES light railway to the Lock L 24 c 8.4 - S.E MARCOING COPSE & L 34 central. A number of stragglers of various units had collected in the Sugar Factory & the wounded also had been collected there. These were all sent off as soon as possible. Still about 8 stretcher cases to go and no stretchers so the Pioneers put handles on Doors as makeshifts. The Reserve Platoon (C coy) was sent off at 10.45 pm with the remainder of the stretcher cases also all men of other units found in the area, chiefly near the Canal.	[illegible]
		11.45	Coys filed out being checked by the Adjutant at the Sugar Factory & by the A/Adjt at the Chateau & the L.F. notified. The Lock Bridge & small foot bridge posts (A coy) went via the Canal & reported to OC R G L I. The rear party 3 men + L.G. under 2nd Lt Parrish could not say definitely that Lock Bridge Post was totally evacuated so 2nd Lt Parrish was sent back with a man to search, while the L.G. was posted at the small foot bridge, 5 men were found & withdrawn & with HQ passed the Chateau at 1.15 am. On the way along light railway one stretcher case R.F. with tired out bearers was picked up and brought in. The evacuation was carried out without any fighting. The men came out complete	[illegible]

WAR DIARY
or
INTELLIGENCE SUMMARY.
(Erase heading not required.)

Army Form C. 2118.

Instructions regarding War Diaries and Intelligence Summaries are contained in F. S. Regs., Part II. and the Staff Manual respectively. Title pages will be prepared in manuscript.

Place	Date	Hour	Summary of Events and Information	Remarks and references to Appendices
			complete with arms & ammunition & very nearly complete with tools. No wounded were left behind & so far as is known no stragglers.	[illegible]
	1st/2nd		Bn occupies trenches about I 34 central (MARCOING)	[illegible]
	2nd		" marches via TRESCAULT to RIBECOURT & is billeted in farm	[illegible]
	3rd	11 am	" left RIBECOURT and occupied Hindenburg Line.	[illegible]
		5.30 pm	" moves from Hindenburg Line to HAVRINCOURT WOOD & is accommodated in tents & bivouacs for the night.	[illegible]
	4th	1 pm	Bn left HAVRINCOURT WOOD & marches to FINS and are billeted in huts.	[illegible]
	5th	12.15 pm	" " FINS & marched to ETRICOURT & entrains at 4.30 pm for PETIT HOUVIN.	[illegible]
	6th	4.30 am	" Detrained at PETIT HOUVIN & marches to MAIZIERES & is billeted in village	[illegible]
	7th/15th		" reorganising and training.	[illegible]
	16th	10 am	" left MAIZIERES & marches via HOUVIN, FRÉVENT, and FLERS to BLANGERMONT.	[illegible]
	17th		" " BLANGERMONT and marches to GRIGNY.	[illegible]
	18th		" " GRIGNY and marches through blizzards & snow drifts a distance of about 15 miles to RENTY, one man only fell out.	[illegible]
	19/31st		Bn billeted in village of RENTY and resumes training.	[illegible]

8353 Wt. W2544/1454 700,000 5/15 D. D. & L. A.D.S.S./Forms/C. 2118.

WAR DIARY
or
INTELLIGENCE SUMMARY.
(Erase heading not required.)

Army Form C. 2118.

[illegible]ions regarding War Diaries and Intelligence [illegible]mmaries are contained in F. S. Regs., Part II. [illegible]nd the Staff Manual respectively. Title pages will be prepared in manuscript.

January 1918 — 1st Middlesex Regt. 29th Division — Volume XXVII — Page 32

Vol 27

Place	Date	Hour	Summary of Events and Information	Remarks and references to Appendices
RENTY	1st–2nd		New Year's Honours.	
			Capt. & Adjt. H. M. James M.C.	
			[illegible] Coy. S. M. R. Scott D.C.M.	
			P.S. 16.C. „ [illegible] Kirk mentioned in despatches	
	4th–12th		Bn. resting and training.	[illegible]
RENTY	13th	[illegible]	Bn. left RENTY and marched via FAUQUEMBERGUES, AIRONT, CLETY and ESQUERDES to SETQUES.	[illegible]
			HQ A.B.C.D. coys billeted in SETQUES. D coy in FERSINGHEM.	
	14th–15th		Bn. and Bde training. Heavy falls of snow and continuous frosts.	[illegible]
SETQUES	16th	4.30am	Bn. left SETQUES and FERSINGHEM marching to and entraining at WIZERNES at 7 am	[illegible]
			Bn. detrained at BRANDHOEK at 10.40 am & marched to RED ROSE CAMP H.1.d.9.7 (Sheet 28 N.W.)	
ST JEAN	17th		Bn. leaves H.1.d.9.7 & marches to ST JEAN via VLAMERTINGHE & YPRES & is accommodated in [illegible] JUNCTION CAMP C.27.c.2.4.	[illegible]
	18th		Bn. less details proceed to reserve line relieving the BERK Regt. with HQ established at MEETCHEELE D.5.c.95.90 D.4.a.8.2 ZONNEBEKE (Sheet 28 N.E.1.) Casualties 1 other rank killed & 1 wounded	[illegible]
[illegible]	19th		Details move from JUNCTION CAMP to CALIFORNIA CAMP (WIELTJE) C.23.c.5.4 (Sheet 28 N.W.).	[illegible]
	19th [illegible]		Bn. relieved in the line by 1st Lancashire Fusrs. & are accommodated in CALIFORNIA CAMP	
	20th–22		Bn. engaged on improvements in CALIFORNIA CAMP.	[illegible]
[illegible]	22nd	4.30p	Bn. less details proceed to the front line & relieve the Lanc. Fusil. with HQrs. established at [illegible] BOX [illegible] in D.4.b.2.3.	[illegible]
[illegible]EK	23rd–25th		Bn. in the line. Details with Transport at BRANDHOEK. Casualties 1 OR killed, 1 wounded 2 missing	[illegible]
	26th		Bn. relieved by 2nd Hants & entrain at WIELTJE at 1.15 am (27th) detraining at BRANDHOEK and marches to RED ROSE CAMP.	
[illegible]INGHE	27th–31st		Bn. resting and working on Camp improvements.	[illegible]
			HONOURS & AWARDS received for operations during the CAMBRAI offensive.	

Capt. [illegible] attd. 2nd Bn. [illegible] M.C. — 2170 Sgt. [illegible] D.C.M. — 153178 Pte. G. H. Turner M.M.
Capt. W. H. [illegible] Bar to M.C. — 1781 „ [illegible] — 51081 „ J. F. Jones „
2/Lt. [illegible] M.C. — [illegible] Pte. [illegible] M.M. — 20928 L/Cpl. [illegible] „
2/Lt. [illegible] „ — 235[illegible] „ [illegible] „ — 3[illegible]02 „ R. March „ Border Regt. attd. 16th [illegible]
„ A. G. [illegible] „ — 52341 „ [illegible] „
„ D. O. [illegible] „ — [illegible] L/Cpl. [illegible] Turner „
„ A. H. [illegible] „ — 40324 Pte. [illegible] Simmons „

2353 Wt. W2544/1454 700,000 5/15 D. D. & L. A.D.S.S./Forms/C. 2118.

Instructions regarding War Diaries and Intelligence Summaries are contained in F. S. Regs., Part II. and the Staff Manual respectively. Title pages will be prepared in manuscript.

WAR DIARY
or
INTELLIGENCE SUMMARY.

(Erase heading not required.)

Army Form C. 2118.

February 1918.

16th Middlesex Regt.
29th Division.
Volume XXVIII Page 33.

29

Place	Date	Hour	Summary of Events and Information	Remarks and references to Appendices
	1.2.18.		Battalion in RED ROSE CAMP	
	3.2.18.		Battalion moves to JUNCTION CAMP by light railway from BRANDHOEK detraining at St JEAN for work on GRAVENSTAFEL Line.	
			Orders received to disband the Battalion.	
	4.2.18.		Battalion Hd Qrs move to WARRINGTON CAMP	
	4/6		Battalion in JUNCTION CAMP.	
	5th		"D" Coy join Battn Hd Qrs in WARRINGTON CAMP.	
			"A" " " " " " "	
	7th		B & C Coys " " " " " "	
	8th		Draft of 14 Officers + 275 other ranks made up from "D" Coy and 2 platoons of "A" Coy transferred to 18th Middlesex march to POPERINGHE + entrain at 11.15am for WIZERNES.	
			Draft of 7 Officers + 150 other ranks "C" Coy transferred to 2nd Middlesex embus at WARRINGTON CAMP at 11.30am and proceed to WINNIZEELE.	
	11th		Draft of 14 Officers + 274 other ranks made up from "B" Coy and balance of "A" + "C" Coys transferred to 20th Middlesex march to VLAMERTINGHE and entrain at 10.30am for ACHIET.	
			Transport - strength 1 Officer + 46 other ranks - move from BRANDHOEK to NINE ELMS CAMP	
			Battalion Hd Qrs and details - strength 3 Officers + 58 other ranks - march to VIIIth Corps	

2353 Wt. W2544/1454 700,000 5/15 D. D. & L. A.D.S.S./Forms/C. 2118.

Instructions regarding War Diaries and Intelligence Summaries are contained in F. S. Regs., Part II. and the Staff Manual respectively. Title pages will be prepared in manuscript.

(Sheet 2)

WAR DIARY
or
INTELLIGENCE SUMMARY.

(Erase heading not required.)

Army Form C. 2118.

Place	Date	Hour	Summary of Events and Information	Remarks and references to Appendices
	11th (contd)		Reinforcement Camp POPERINGHE	
			Disbandment of Battalion complete.	
	12th		Details accommodated in VIIIth Corps Rest Station. Hd Qrs established in Rue de Bruges.	
			1 other rank proceeded to England (Candidate for Temporary Commission)	
	13th		14 other ranks (Casuals) despatched to 18th Middlesex	
			1 other rank proceeded to England (Candidate for T.C.)	
	14.		Honours won in CAMBRAI Battle.	
			Lt Col. J. Forbes. Robertson D.S.O. M.C. awarded bar to D.S.O.	
			2/Lt. J. W. Deeves. M.C. " " " M.C.	
			Capt. B. Knowles (RAMC) attached 16th Middlesex awarded M.C.	
	22nd		Lieut. Col. J. Forbes. Robertson D.S.O.MC. proceeds to join 1st BORDER Regt.	

Major.
Commdg: 16th Middlesex Regt.

#353 Wt. W2544/1454 700,000 5/15 D. D. & L. A.D.S.S./Forms/C. 2118.

16th BATTALION THE MIDDLESEX REGIMENT.
29th DIVISION.

1918.

February.		Appendix.
1st.	Battalion in RED ROSE CAMP.	
3rd.	Battalion moves to JUNCTION CAMP by light railway from BRANDHOEK detraining at ST.JEAN for work on GRAVENSTAFEL Line. Orders received to disband the Battalion.	
4th.	Battalion Hd.Qrs. to WARRINGTON CAMP.	
4th/6th.	Battalion in JUNCTION CAMP.	
5th.	"D" Coy.join Battn.Hd.Qrs.in WARRINGTON CAMP. "A" Coy.join Battn.Hd.Qrs.in WARRINGTON CAMP.	
7th.	"B" & "C" Coys. join Battn.Hd. Qrs. in WARRINGTON CAMP.	
8th.	Draft of 14 Officers & 275 Other Ranks made up from "D" Coy. and 2 platoons of "A" Coy. transferred to 18th Middlesex march to POPERINGHE & entrain at 11.15 a.m. for WIZERNES. Draft of 7 Officers & 150 other ranks "C" Coy. transferred to 2nd Middlesex embus at WARRINGTON CAMP at 11.30 am. and proceed to WINNIZEELE.	
11th.	Draft of 14 Officers & 274 Other Ranks made up from "B" Coy. and balance of "A" & "C" Coys. transferred to 20th Middlesex march to VLAMERTINGHE and entrain at 10.30 am. for ACHIET. Transport - strength 1 Officer & 46 Other Ranks - move from BRANDHOEK to NINE ELMS CAMP Battalion Hd.Qrs. and details - strength 3 Officers & 58 Other Ranks - march to VIIIth Corps. Reinforcement Camp POPERINGHE. Disbandment of Battalion complete.	

1918.

February. Appendix.

12th. Details accommodated in VIIIth Corps Rest Station. Hd.Qrs. established in Rue de Bruges. 1 Other Rank proceeded to England (Candidate for Temporary commission).

13th. 14 Other Ranks (Casuals) despatched to 18th Middlesex. 1 other rank proceeded to England (Candidate for T.C.)

14th. Honours won in CAMBRAI Battle.
Lt.Col. J. Forbes-Robertson, D.S.O. M.C. awarded bar to D.S.O.
2.Lt. T.W. Deeves M.C. awarded bar to M.C.
Capt. B. Knowles (R.A.M.C) attached 16th Middlesex awarded M.C.

22nd. Lieut.Col. J. Forbes-Robertson D.S.O, M.C. proceeds to join 1st BORDER REGT.

Major,
Commdg. 16th Middlesex Regt.

16th BATTALION THE MIDDLESEX REGIMENT.
29th DIVISION.

1918.

February. Appendix.

1st.	Battalion in RED ROSE CAMP.
3rd.	Battalion moves to JUNCTION CAMP by light railway from BRANDHOEK detraining at ST.JEAN for work on GRAVENSTAFEL Line. Orders received to disband the Battalion.
4th.	Battalion Hd.Qrs. to WARRINGTON CAMP.
4th/6th.	Battalion in JUNCTION CAMP.
5th.	"D" Coy.join Battn.Hd.Qrs.in WARRINGTON CAMP. "A" Coy.join Battn.Hd.Qrs.in WARRINGTON CAMP.
7th.	"B" & "C" Coys. join Battn.Hd. Qrs. in WARRINGTON CAMP.
8th.	Draft of 14 Officers & 275 Other Ranks made up from "D" Coy. and 2 platoons of "A" Coy. transferred to 18th Middlesex march to POPERINGHE & entrain at 11.15 a.m. for WIZERNES. Draft of 7 Officers & 150 other ranks "C" Coy. transferred to 2nd Middlesex embus at WARRINGTON CAMP at 11.30 am. and proceed to WINNIZEELE.
11th.	Draft of 14 Officers & 274 Other Ranks made up from "B" Coy. and balance of "A" & "C" Coys. transferred to 20th Middlesex march to VLAMERTINGHE and entrain at 10.30 am. for ACHIET. Transport - strength 1 Officer & 46 Other Ranks - move from BRANDHOEK to NINE ELMS CAMP Battalion Hd.Qrs. and details - strength 3 Officers & 58 Other Ranks - march to VIIIth Corps. Reinforcement Camp POPERINGHE. Disbandment of Battalion complete.

1918.

February. Appendix.

12th.	Details accommodated in VIIIth Corps Rest Station. Hd.Qrs. established in Rue de Bruges. 1 Other Rank proceeded to England (Candidate for Temporary commission).
13th.	14 Other Ranks (Casuals) despatched to 18th Middlesex. 1 other rank proceeded to England (Candidate for T.C.)
14th.	Honours won in CAMBRAI Battle. Lt.Col. J. Forbes-Robertson, D.S.O. M.C. awarded bar to D.S.O. 2.Lt. T.W. Deeves M.C. awarded bar to M.C. Capt. B. Knowles (R.A.M.C) attached 16th Middlesex awarded M.C.
22nd.	Lieut.Col. J. Forbes-Robertson D.S.O, M.C. proceeds to join 1st BORDER REGT.

Major,
Commdg. 16th Middlesex Regt.

16th BATTALION THE MIDDLESEX REGIMENT.
29th DIVISION.

1918.

February.		**Appendix.**
1st.	Battalion in RED ROSE CAMP.	
3rd.	Battalion moves to JUNCTION CAMP by light railway from BRANDHOEK detraining at ST.JEAN for work on GRAVENSTAFEL Line. Orders received to disband the Battalion.	
4th.	Battalion Hd.Qrs. to WARRINGTON CAMP.	
4th/6th.	Battalion in JUNCTION CAMP.	
5th.	"D" Coy.join Battn.Hd.Qrs.in WARRINGTON CAMP. "A" Coy.join Battn.Hd.Qrs.in WARRINGTON CAMP.	
7th.	"B" & "C" Coys. join Battn.Hd. Qrs. in WARRINGTON CAMP.	
8th.	Draft of 14 Officers & 275 Other Ranks made up from "D" Coy. and 2 platoons of "A" Coy. transferred to 18th Middlesex march to POPERINGHE & entrain at 11.15 a.m. for WIZERNES. Draft of 7 Officers & 150 other ranks "C" Coy. transferred to 2nd Middlesex embus at WARRINGTON CAMP at 11.30 am. and proceed to WINNIZEELE.	
11th.	Draft of 14 Officers & 274 Other Ranks made up from "B" Coy. and balance of "A" & "C" Coys. transferred to 20th Middlesex march to VLAMERTINGHE and entrain at 10.30 am. for ACHIET. Transport - strength 1 Officer & 46 Other Ranks - move from BRANDHOEK to NINE ELMS CAMP Battalion Hd.Qrs. and details - strength 3 Officers & 58 Other Ranks - march to VIIIth Corps. Reinforcement Camp POPERINGHE. Disbandment of Battalion complete.	

1918.

February. Appendix.

12th.	Details accommodated in VIIIth Corps Rest Station. Hd.Qrs. established in Rue de Bruges. 1 Other Rank proceeded to England (Candidate for Temporary commission).
13th.	14 Other Ranks (Casuals) despatched to 18th Middlesex. 1 other rank proceeded to England (Candidate for T.C.)
14th.	Honours won in CAMBRAI Battle. Lt.Col. J. Forbes-Robertson, D.S.O. M.C. awarded bar to D.S.O. 2.Lt. T.W. Deeves M.C. awarded bar to M.C. Capt. B. Knowles (R.A.M.C) attached 16th Middlesex awarded M.C.
22nd.	Lieut.Col. J. Forbes-Robertson D.S.O, M.C. proceeds to join 1st BORDER REGT.

Major,
Commdg. 16th Middlesex Regt.

www.ingramcontent.com/pod-product-compliance
Lightning Source LLC
Chambersburg PA
CBHW081239170426
43191CB00034B/1977
* 9 7 8 1 4 7 4 5 1 4 7 8 1 *